How Public Schools Really Work

How Public Schools Really Work

An Insider's Guide for Parents and Practitioners

Parry Graham

ROWMAN & LITTLEFIELD
Lanham • Boulder • New York • London

Published by Rowman & Littlefield
An imprint of The Rowman & Littlefield Publishing Group, Inc.
4501 Forbes Boulevard, Suite 200, Lanham, Maryland 20706
www.rowman.com

86-90 Paul Street, London EC2A 4NE, United Kingdom

Copyright © 2022 by Parry Graham

All rights reserved. No part of this book may be reproduced in any form or by any electronic or mechanical means, including information storage and retrieval systems, without written permission from the publisher, except by a reviewer who may quote passages in a review.

British Library Cataloguing in Publication Information Available

Library of Congress Cataloging-in-Publication Data Available

ISBN 9781475867145 (cloth) | ISBN 9781475867152 (paper) | ISBN 9781475867169 (epub)

To Betsy, Sydney, and Jared—you gave me the year I needed to write this, and the encouragement I needed to finish it.

Contents

Acknowledgments	xi
Author page	xiii
Introduction	xv

SECTION 1: TEACHERS: WHY NOTHING IS MORE IMPORTANT THAN HAVING A GOOD ONE — 1

1 How Do You Spot and Take Advantage of a Good Teacher? — 3
- (1) Good Teachers Care — 4
- (2) Good Teachers Are Organized — 4
- (3) Good Teachers Set Big Goals for Their Kids and for Themselves — 4
- (4) Good Teachers Provide Lots of Feedback — 5
- (5) Good Teachers Have Deep Content Knowledge — 5
- (6) Good Teachers Are With-It — 6
- Taking Advantage of a Good Teacher — 6

2 How Do You Get a Good Teacher for Your Child? — 9
- Know Your Child — 10
- Know the Teachers — 10
- Provide Information, Not Requests — 12
- Understand the Differences between Elementary, Middle, and High Schools — 13

3 How Do You Make the Best of an Average Teacher? — 17
- Build a Good Relationship — 18
- Learn about the Curriculum — 19
- Monitor Your Child's Progress — 21

4	**How Do You Work with a Teacher about a Question or Concern?**	**25**
	• Be Polite	25
	• Seek to Understand	26
	• Be Clear and Specific	27
	• Use E-mail Carefully	27
	• Don't Get Your Child Involved	28
	• Pick Your Battles	29
	• Involve Administration as a Last Resort	29
5	**How Do You Handle a Truly Bad Teacher?**	**31**
	• Personnel Practices in Public Education: The Good, the Bad, and the Ugly	31
	• What Parents Can Do about Ineffective Teachers	33

SECTION 2: STUDENT DISCIPLINE: WHY THE SCHOOL BUS IS LIKE *LORD OF THE FLIES* — 45

6	**How Do Schools Deal with Student Discipline**	**47**
	• A Practical Example of a Disciplinary Incident	47
	• How the School Discipline Process Works	50
7	**What Are Common Disciplinary Consequences and What Do They Mean for Students?**	**59**
	• The Range of Disciplinary Consequences	59
	• This Will (Most Likely Not) Go Down on Your Permanent Record	65
8	**Your Child Got Into Trouble with a Teacher—Now What?**	**69**
	• Understand the Situation and the Concern	69
	• Listen to Your Child	71
	• Work with the Teacher	72
	• Escalate when Necessary	75
9	**Your Child Got Into Trouble with an Administrator—Now What?**	**79**
	• Understand the Facts and the Process	79
	• Support Your Child and Work with the School	82
	• Dealing with Especially Serious Situations	88
10	**Your Child Got Into Trouble and You Think the School Screwed Up—What Do You Do?**	**93**
	• You Think Your Child Is Innocent	93
	• You Think the School Screwed Up the Process	94
	• You Think the Consequences Are Excessive	98

Contents

11 Your Child Is a Victim—What Do You Do?   101
- Your Child Is a Victim of Another Student's Behavior, and the School Is Unaware   101
- Your Child Is a Victim of Another Student's Behavior in a School-Investigated Situation   107
- Your Child Is the Victim of a School Staff Member's Behavior   110

SECTION 3: PARENT INVOLVEMENT: WHY PARENTS ARE A SCHOOL'S QUALITY CONTROL   115

12 You Want to Help Out—How Can You Add Value *within* the System?   117
- Examples of What Adding Value Looks Like   117
- How to Find Opportunities to Add Value   120
- How to Make Your Contribution Truly Valuable   123

13 You Want to Help the System Get Better—How Can Parents be a School's Quality Control?   129
- Seek to Understand How the Current System Works   130
- Know What Is—and Isn't—Your Lane   133
- Find and Make Allies   139
- Figure Out Where You Draw the Line   142

Section 1 Appendix   149

Section 2 Appendix   161

Section 3 Appendix   165

Acknowledgments

This book has benefitted from the thoughts, conversations, and feedback of many people. My wife, Betsy, has spent years listening to me talk about the ideas in here and countless hours reading through the many drafts. I owe a debt of gratitude to Eric Schwab, Ed Dehoratius, and Nicolas Rochoux for their feedback and encouragement. I would like to thank the team at Rowman & Littlefield, in particular Tom Koerner, who helped to keep the project alive despite the pandemic. Bien sûr, un grand merci à mes amis Au Point Central à Lille.

Finally, I would like to thank the thousands of educators and parents with whom I have had the privilege to work over the years. This book is a culmination of the time spent with them and the lessons I have learned with and from them.

Author page

Parry Graham is the assistant superintendent of Wayland Public Schools in Wayland, Massachusetts. He began his career in public education in 1994 as a high school teacher and has spent the last seventeen years in leadership roles at the elementary, middle school, high school, and central office levels. He is the coauthor of two previous books: *Making Teamwork Meaningful: Leading Progress-Driven Collaboration in a PLC at Work* in 2013; and *Building a Professional Learning Community at Work: A Guide to the First Year*, which won Learning Forward's 2010 Book of the Year award. Parry completed his doctorate at UNC-Chapel Hill, where he also worked part-time as a clinical assistant professor in the School of Education.

Introduction

Many years ago, my wife and I were out at dinner with another couple. Their daughter had just finished her kindergarten year, and at one point during the evening the husband turned to me with a question.

"Parry, you're a principal—what do we do if we're not happy with the way our daughter's school year went?" He paused a moment, shrugging his shoulders in resignation. "It's not like it was a bad year, it's just that everything felt kind of . . . mediocre. I talked about it with other parents, but nobody knows what to do. What do you think—how do we make next year better?"

Since March of 2020, parents across the United States have gained an unprecedented peek into their children's schools and classrooms. In many cases, this has led to a newfound respect and appreciation for the hard work of teachers and administrators. But in other cases, it has raised concerns. Throughout all of this heightened interest in our public education system, I have often thought back on my friend's question.

If you're reading this book, chances are you're like my friend. You care about your child's education, and you want to do whatever you can to help your child get the best education possible. But you're not sure what "whatever you can" looks like in practice.

Maybe you're unhappy with your child's teacher, but you're hesitant to raise a stink. Maybe you raised a stink, and nothing changed. Maybe you're concerned that your child is being bullied, but he's begged you not to tell. Maybe you told, and things got worse.

As a former principal, I appreciate parents like my friend and like you. I hope for parents who set high expectations and then work as partners with their school to meet those expectations. I hope for parents who expect a quality education in a safe environment and then work themselves to create a supportive environment for their kids at home.

This is the book that I wish my friend, and every one of the parents in my schools, would read. I have worked in public education for over twenty-five years at the elementary, middle, and high school levels. And in every one of my jobs, at every one of my schools, I encountered parents just like my friend: parents who cared deeply about their children, who wanted their children to learn and succeed, but who didn't always know how to work productively with their schools and teachers to get the best possible results.

This book is a collection of insider information, not to help you beat the system, but to help you work with the system—and to make sure the system works with you. Schools want the best for your child, but schools are complex, messy, and imperfect organizations. This book is about how to be patient with the small stuff, how to be serious with the serious stuff, and how to recognize the difference between the two.

ORGANIZATION OF THE BOOK

The book is organized into three parts, each focusing on a different theme: teachers, student discipline, and parent involvement.

Each part contains multiple chapters, geared to provide you with the information you need to understand how your child's school works, and how you can work with your child's school. There is no right or wrong way to read the book. You may want to jump directly to a chapter that addresses a challenge or question you're facing. Or you may want to start at the beginning and read until the end, looking for helpful information along the way.

Here is a quick description of each part, and the chapters that those parts contain. That will help you decide the best way *you* can use the book.

Teachers

The first part of the book looks at the most important part of your child's education: classroom teachers. The chapters in this part of the book address the following questions:

- *Chapter 1:* "How Do You Spot and Take Advantage of a Good Teacher?" This chapter looks at the traits that define good teaching and provides advice on how to take advantage of a year with a good teacher.
- *Chapter 2:* "How Do You Get a Good Teacher for Your Child?" While most schools will likely not let you simply request a specific teacher, this chapter provides advice on ways to help get your child a teacher who will

be a good "fit." The chapter also discusses the difference between getting a good teacher at the elementary, middle, and high school levels.
- *Chapter 3:* "How Do You Make the Best of an Average Teacher?" Not every teacher is a rock star but a year with an average teacher can still be a good year. This chapter looks at strategies to get the best out of a year with an average teacher.
- *Chapter 4:* "How Do You Work with a Teacher about a Question or Concern?" When you have a concern, there are effective and ineffective ways to try to address it with your child's teacher. This chapter will walk you through how to be politely productive.
- *Chapter 5:* "How Do You Handle a Truly Bad Teacher?" Unfortunately, truly bad teachers do exist. If your child is unfortunate enough to have one, this chapter will walk you through how to mitigate any possible damage to your child's education.

Student Discipline

The next section of the book is about student discipline: how schools try to manage student behavior, and what parents can do to support their children in the process. If your child gets into trouble at school, or if your child is a victim of someone else's behavior, this section of the book will help you know what to do. The chapters in this section of the book address the following questions:

- *Chapter 6:* "How Do Schools Deal with Student Discipline?" This is a behind-the-scenes look at how schools handle student discipline, beginning with a real-life example. The chapter discusses topics such as due process, search and seizure, and the role of police in student discipline.
- *Chapter 7:* "What Are Common Disciplinary Consequences and What Do They Mean for Students?" This chapter looks at the typical range of consequences that a student might encounter, and the types of behaviors that might lead to them. It also discusses how schools track student behavior and report disciplinary information to outside institutions.
- *Chapter 8:* "Your Child Got into Trouble with a Teacher—Now What?" It's not uncommon for students to experience some type of classroom-level discipline with a teacher. This chapter helps you deal with it if it happens, with special advice on how to handle any concerns you might have.
- *Chapter 9:* "Your Child Got into Trouble with an Administrator—Now What?" Administrator-level discipline can be more consequential, ranging anywhere from an after-school detention to long-term suspension or expulsion. This chapter helps you understand how administrator-discipline works, and how you can support your child in the process.

- *Chapter 10:* "Your Child Got into Trouble and You Think the School Screwed Up—What Do You Do?" School administrators aren't above making mistakes, and parents have options if they think a disciplinary situation has been mishandled. This chapter will help you advocate for your child if you think their situation was handled inappropriately.
- *Chapter 11:* "Your Child Is a Victim—What Do You Do?" Unfortunately, kids can treat each other badly at times. This chapter will help you know what to do if your child is a victim of someone else's behavior, including a staff member's inappropriate conduct.

Parent Involvement

The final section of the book looks at how parents can add quality to their child's school while also serving as a quality control. The chapters in this section of the book address the following questions:

- *Chapter 12:* "You Want to Help Out—How Can You Add Value *within* the System?" Parents can be a huge asset to a school, volunteering time, expertise, and financial support. This chapter will help you figure out ways that you can be involved, providing advice on how to find and make the most out of the right opportunity.
- *Chapter 13:* "You Want to Help the System Get Better—How Can Parents Be a School's Quality Control?" The book's final chapter walks you through how to address a frustration or concern that you have with your child's school or district. It will help you understand what is and isn't your "lane," share advice on how to find allies in making a change, and talk through what to do when nothing seems to work.

FINAL NOTES

Before you dive in, there are a couple final notes about the book. The first two are about language.

Throughout the book, the terms "parent" and "parents" are used frequently, but those terms are meant very broadly. Children can be raised by a wide range of caregivers: biological parents, legal guardians, adopted parents, a grandparent, a foster parent, and so on. When the word "parent" is used, it means anyone operating in the role of a formal caregiver for a child.

The book also switches interchangeably between referring to male and female students. In some instances, there may be generalized, gender-based patterns that are highlighted, but the rest of the time the intent is simply to try to be inclusive in the use of gender-specific pronouns. So, when the pronouns *he*, *she*, or *they* are used, the intent is not to draw attention to a specific gender.

The book also uses a variety of stories to provide concrete examples of more abstract ideas or advice. All of the stories in the book are drawn from actual situations that occurred, but in most cases enough details have been changed that the real-life people who formed the basis of the stories would not be able to recognize themselves. The intent is to provide an accurate look at what happens in schools, while also protecting people's privacy.

Finally, this is a book that is grounded in lived experiences. In various places, there will be references to educational research, but the intent is not to give the reader a dissertation. Instead, the goal is for you to have an accurate, readable, experience-based guide to the realities of how public schools work.

Section 1

TEACHERS

WHY NOTHING IS MORE IMPORTANT THAN HAVING A GOOD ONE

It's a simple truth: at your child's school, nothing is more important than the quality of the teachers. Tons of educational research support the fact that good teachers are worth their weight in gold.[1] One research study even suggests that the students of good kindergarten teachers can end up earning hundreds of thousands of dollars more in their lifetimes than the students of lousy kindergarten teachers.[2]

That means that, if your child has good teachers, chances are your child will have a good school year. Unfortunately, the reverse is also true: bad teachers can very well lead to a bad year.

This section is all about teachers—knowing when a teacher is great, average, or bottom of the barrel—and knowing how to handle each of those scenarios. Chapter 1 focuses on the characteristics that make good teachers "good" and then provides some advice on how to take advantage of years with a good teacher. Chapter 2 looks at how to work with your school to try to get the best possible teacher(s) for your child.

Chapters 3, 4, and 5 shift to the not-so-stellar situations. Chapter 3 discusses the ways to get the best out of a year with an average teacher, while chapter 4 provides suggestions on how to work effectively with a teacher when you have a question or concern. Finally, chapter 5 talks about the worst-case scenario: what to do when your child has a truly lousy teacher.

NOTES

1. There are many scholarly studies that connect quality of teaching to student learning. A few include Darling-Hammond, L. (2000). Teacher quality and student achievement: A review of state policy evidence. *Education Policy Analysis Archives*,

8(1). Retrieved May 26, 2005, from http://epaa.asu.edu/epaa/v8n1/; Sanders, W. L., & Rivers, J. C. (1996). Cumulative and residual effects of teachers on future student academic achievement. Knoxville, TN: University of Tennessee; Wenglinsky, H. (2002). How schools matter: The link between teacher classroom practices and student academic performance. *Education Policy Analysis Archives, 10*(12). Retrieved May 13, 2003, from http:// epaa.asu.edu/epaa/v10n12/; and Wright, S. P., Horn, S. P., & Sanders, W. L. (1997). Teacher and classroom context effects on student achievement: Implications for teacher evaluation. *Journal of Professional Evaluation, 11*: 57–67.

2. Shortly after it came out, there were articles about this study in multiple publications, such as the *New York Times* ("The Case for $320,000 Kindergarten Teachers"). The actual study is Chetty, R., Friedman, J. N., Hilger, N., Saez, E., Schanzenbach, D., & Yagan, D. (2010). *How does your kindergarten classroom affect your earnings?: Evidence from Project STAR*. Retrieved February 26, 2013, from http://www.cas.umt.edu/econ/faculty/members/bookwalter/documents/w16381.pdf.

Chapter 1

How Do You Spot and Take Advantage of a Good Teacher?

It's actually not that simple to figure out if your child has a "good" teacher. Some of the traits that parents might initially hone in on—personality, educational background, or years of experience—actually have little to do with teacher quality. "Nice" teachers can be lousy, while "strict" teachers can be outstanding, and vice versa.

The truth is, good teaching is complex, as much art as it is science. But there are common traits that good teachers share, even if their individual styles look different. The following list is informed by research on effective teaching, along with real-life observations of hundreds of teachers.

1. Good teachers care.
2. Good teachers are organized.
3. Good teachers set big goals for their kids and for themselves.
4. Good teachers provide lots of feedback.
5. Good teachers have deep content knowledge.
6. Good teachers are with-it.

The coming pages provide more detailed information about these traits. But there are also some resources you can use in the appendix. There you will find vignettes that show what these traits can look like in practice, along with a checklist that will help you determine how "good" your child's teacher is. So, if you're reading through the following information and you want some concrete examples, look for those resources in the appendix.

(1) GOOD TEACHERS CARE

Good teachers care about their kids, plain and simple. This can look very different from grade to grade and from teacher to teacher: a caring kindergarten teacher may be sweet and bubbly, whereas a caring high school teacher might seem strict and demanding. But however it manifests itself, good teachers care.

Caring matters for a lot of reasons, but one really stands out: a teacher who cares builds relationships with kids, and this helps her be a more effective instructor. When students feel positively about a teacher, they are more likely to be motivated in the class, to be engaged, and to do their best work. Just like an adult can work harder because he likes his boss, a student can work harder because he likes his teacher.

(2) GOOD TEACHERS ARE ORGANIZED

Effective organization is at the heart of effective teaching. Good teachers have systems in place, know what they're doing each day, have clear routines and procedures, and keep track of their kids' work, progress, and grades.

Organization is important for a variety of reasons. Systems and routines help a teacher to maximize efficiency and *time on task*, which is edu-speak for "time spent focused on doing work." Clear, consistent classroom structures allow students to quickly get to work, to minimize disruptions and transitions, and to anticipate possible hurdles. Curricular organization means that lessons are sequenced in logical ways, and concepts build on each other in complexity.

(3) GOOD TEACHERS SET BIG GOALS FOR THEIR KIDS AND FOR THEMSELVES

Good teachers are ambitious. They believe that their students can accomplish big things, and they believe that hard work—both the students' and their own—is what will lead to success. This is a hugely important trait. Students who believe that they will succeed or fail based on their intelligence are likely to give up when tasks or assignments become difficult: they figure they must not be smart enough to accomplish them. But students who believe that success is a product of hard work will keep plugging away, even when the going gets tough—they are convinced that, if they work hard enough, they can succeed.

Likewise, teachers who set big goals for their students are more likely to work hard themselves and to persevere when students might struggle. They will push kids to succeed, and students respond because they know their teacher believes in them.

(4) GOOD TEACHERS PROVIDE LOTS OF FEEDBACK

Good teachers let students know how they are progressing by giving them lots of feedback. Feedback can be provided in many different ways: it can be notes on an essay, verbal comments in class, a scored rubric attached to a project, or electronic edits on a term paper. One quick example: effective math teachers might give their kids small whiteboards and, as they call out problems, the kids solve them on the whiteboards, hold up the boards with their answers, and then the teacher is able to immediately see (and give feedback on) how everyone in the class is doing.

Regular and ongoing feedback may be the most important pedagogical strategy used by good teachers because it is so critical to the learning process. Think about your own personal learning experiences as an adult—maybe taking a cooking class, studying a foreign language, or learning a new software program for work. Getting ongoing feedback from an expert allowed you to correct mistakes and gradually improve.

Appropriate feedback helps students make the small steps every day that add up to a great year, and good feedback allows students to experience the type of success that is highly motivating. It's one of the reasons children love video games: they receive constant feedback about their performance, they get a little bit better each time they play, and the game gets incrementally harder so that it stays challenging and exciting.

(5) GOOD TEACHERS HAVE DEEP CONTENT KNOWLEDGE

Good teachers know their subject areas. This is especially evident in high school, where students study some pretty advanced concepts, but it's also important in the younger grades. Teachers who really know their content area have a strong sense of how to structure a curriculum, how to tie different concepts together, and how to answer the inevitable, non-scripted questions that are a part of any vibrant classroom.

Deep content knowledge, however, does not just mean knowing the content itself. It also means knowing how to *teach* the content to students. Some educators are brilliant in their subject areas, but they become easily frustrated when students don't quickly grasp the concepts and ideas that are so obvious to them. Good teachers know where students will have a hard time, they know tricks to help make difficult content make sense, and they know how to connect content to students' lives and interests.

(6) GOOD TEACHERS ARE WITH-IT

Good teachers have eyes in the backs of their heads; they have an intuitive ability to "read" the moods, personalities, and behaviors of their students, and they have a presence, an ability to command the attention and respect of the class.

"With-itness" is important because it connects to a teacher's ability to engage and motivate students and to effectively manage student behavior. Teachers who lack this quality will struggle to keep students in line and will have higher incidences of discipline problems. They will also lose valuable learning time as they constantly have to put out silly fires. In contrast, teachers who *are* with-it keep their rooms running smoothly, freeing up their attention to focus on student progress and not student behavior.

TAKING ADVANTAGE OF A GOOD TEACHER

As you read through the qualities that define good teachers, one hopes that you found that your child's teacher possesses many, if not all, of them. If not, the next couple of chapters will help you deal with a not-so-great teacher.

But if you were reading that list thinking, "This sounds exactly like my child's teacher!" then you want to do everything you can to take advantage of a good year.

Here are some suggestions to help you get the best out of the good times:

- Reinforce at home what your child enjoys at school—Really good teachers tend to bring out specific interests in kids, especially as children get older. Whether it's a budding humanitarian streak, an obsession with national monuments, or a new interest in computer programming, your child's expanding interests mean something to him—tap into and support those passions outside of school.

  This might mean checking out books by a new favorite author, scheduling a family trip to the local art museum, signing up for an after-school club, or letting your child help with the grocery shopping. As children get older, they are trying to figure out who they are, and good teachers will spark new interests. Support those interests, and you are supporting your

child's maturation and development, even if the new passion lasts only a short time.
- Get to know your child through the teacher's eyes—It is a truism that parents know their children better than anyone else, but parents tend to know their children in certain contexts. Teachers have experience working with hundreds, maybe even thousands of different kids. They are in the unique position of being able to describe your child in comparison to other children and being able to describe your child in a social and academic context that you usually don't see. When you talk to your child's teacher, listen with an open mind about who your child is becoming as a student and as a social being. Also pay attention to what their teacher says about your child's areas of strength and weakness.
- Support the teacher—Being a bad teacher may be one of the easiest jobs in the world, but being a good teacher has got to be one of the toughest. Bad teachers tend to do the bare minimum, whereas good teachers work their tails off. Supporting a good teacher helps her do her job a little bit better: volunteering in the classroom, buying classroom supplies, chaperoning a band trip, or organizing a teacher appreciation luncheon are all examples of ways to make her job a little bit easier (leaving more time and energy for the students) and to give her a little boost of enthusiasm.

Chapter 2

How Do You Get a Good Teacher for Your Child?

It's pretty common for principals to get requests from parents for their child to have a specific teacher. But any school administrator worth his or her salt will ignore these sorts of requests.

When hearing this, parents sometimes ask why. "What's the harm in just letting parents pick the teachers they want?" they say. The brief answer is that school administrators aren't just responsible for *your* child, they are responsible for *all* the children in the school. If administrators allow parents to pick their children's teachers, some parents are going to have an advantage because some parents are more "in the know" about who the best teachers are. If administrators allow parents to pick the teachers they want, kids won't have equal access to good teachers.

This means that, when you ask the principal to make sure your child has a specific teacher, you should expect that answer to be "I'm sorry, we don't make teacher assignments based on parent request."

But that doesn't mean that you are entirely powerless in determining who teaches your child. Most schools (hopefully all schools) want to make the best matches possible between students and teachers. This is especially true at the elementary level. And that means that they are likely to solicit, or at least accept, parent feedback as part of the assignment process. Whether they ask for it or simply accept it, you have the opportunity to help influence your child's teacher assignments.

To do that you need to:

- Know your child
- Know the teachers
- Provide information, not requests
- Understand the differences between elementary, middle, and high schools.

KNOW YOUR CHILD

There are plenty of teachers out there who are really popular with some students and parents but really unpopular with others. It's not impossible to have the same high school teacher be one child's favorite, having a huge, positive impact on the kid's choice of major in college, while also being another student's worst nightmare, responsible for countless frustrated and tearful nights.

The point is, even among "good" teachers, there are teachers who are better and worse matches for different kids. What you want to find is a good teacher who is also a good "fit" for your child.

The first step of getting that good "fit" is thinking about who your child is as a student in as objective a way possible. We would all like to believe that our children are perfect angels with unlimited potential, but for the purposes of thinking about a teacher match, it helps to think more realistically. Consider these questions as you reflect on your child's "student" personality:

- What have previous teachers said about your child's academic strengths and weaknesses?
- What have previous teachers said about your child's classroom behavior?
- In terms of your own parenting style, what does your child tend to respond to best?
- When looking for activities to engage in during free time, does your child need clear direction and instructions to use free time well, or is he able to come up with activities independently to keep himself engaged?
- Do you see your child demonstrate any preferences in terms of the gender of her teacher? Does she tend to work better with female teachers, with male teachers, or does it not seem to matter?
- Does your child tend to be intellectually curious, asking lots of questions and delving independently into various subjects? Or, does your child tend to prefer routines and rules, with clear expectations and tasks? (e.g., does your child like to pick his own book to read, or be told what he should read?)
- Is your child relatively emotionally independent, or does she tend to need lots of affirmation and emotional support to feel comfortable?

KNOW THE TEACHERS

In addition to having an objective sense of who your child is as a student, you also want to know as much as you can about who the teachers are in your child's school.

There are three general ways to learn about the qualities and personalities of teachers at a school: talk to other parents, meet and interact with the teachers directly, and use school documents or publications. The following tips will help you to use all three, but one important proviso: take the comments of others with a healthy grain of salt. If you hear one parent rave about a teacher or trash a teacher, remember that it's just one opinion. If you start to hear the same thing over and over from multiple parents, however, that's probably something to pay attention to.

- Use extracurriculars to meet other parents—It is amazing how much a parent can learn about a school by talking to other parents during their children's Saturday afternoon soccer games (or field hockey games, or basketball practices at the Y). This lesson doesn't just apply to sports, but sports do tend to provide the perfect opportunity of access to other parents and time to fill. When you meet other parents, make a point of asking them about their experiences with different teachers. Try to be polite and discreet about it—don't start a conversation with "So, who's the best fourth-grade teacher at the school?"—but make a point of asking them what grades their children are in, who they had as teachers, and what their experiences were with those teachers.

  One challenge with sports is that they can be expensive, but there are lots of low-cost extracurriculars that are fun and still provide opportunities for parents to meet each other. Activities through churches or other houses of worship are certainly an option, along with scouting, the local playground, or the town library. The key is to find opportunities to speak with other parents and hear about their experiences and insights (and to share your own).
- Get involved in parent groups—This is another great way to meet other parents and learn about their opinions. Most schools have some sort of parent-teacher association that parents are encouraged to join, and middle and high schools oftentimes have parent groups that support specific school activities, such as band boosters or Turkey Trot organizers. While the formal meetings of these groups will probably not touch directly on discussions of individual teachers, the informal conversations after the formal meetings most certainly can.
- Meet the teachers—When you have opportunities to meet teachers, take advantage of it. Most schools have back-to-school nights when parents can meet their children's own teachers but take advantage of opportunities to meet other teachers as well. When schools have Math Nights or Reading Nights, those can be chances to interact with different teachers. Some schools recognize outstanding teachers at end-of-year awards ceremonies, and savvy parents use that information to identify who they hope their child's teacher will be the next year.

- Volunteer in the school—If you have the time and ability to spend time in your child's school, it can be a great way to get to know the teachers and maybe even to see them in action. If the school is looking for guest readers, guest speakers, or just someone to help prepare for an in-school event, take advantage of opportunities to spend time in the school and in classrooms.
- Ask a teacher friend—If you have a friend who teaches at the school or in the district, they can be a great source of information. Make sure you take their comments with a grain of salt, however—their own personal prejudices could color their opinions—and don't be surprised if they are somewhat cagey in their responses. Teachers with friends who are parents in the same system walk a fine line, and they will typically be diplomatic in their descriptions of their colleagues. But they will generally be happy to say positive things about their respected colleagues, so take effusive praise as likely being genuine.
- Review the school website—School websites may not provide very specific information about teachers, but they can let you know how many teachers there are at a certain grade level or in a certain subject. And teacher accolades are frequently posted on school websites, so they can be a place to learn about the super achievers.
- Subscribe to school newsletters and bulletins—Much like school websites, school newsletters and bulletins are unlikely to have specific information about teachers, but they can highlight different teacher superstars. If you keep reading about the same teacher doing exciting and interesting things, that's probably a name to remember.

PROVIDE INFORMATION, NOT REQUESTS

Having spent some time thinking about your child's personality as a student and learning about the teachers in the school, you next want to provide the school with information that will help them connect the dots.

Remember that an outright teacher request is likely to be ignored, and could actually hurt your chances of your child having a specific teacher. If you tell the school "I have heard that Mrs. Peisner is a great second-grade teacher and I would like my son to have her," you've actually made it difficult for the school to assign your child to this teacher. It could appear that they are granting you a specific request that they are not granting to others.

Instead, you want to provide the school with information about your child that is likely to lead to a good match, and that allows the school to make that match without feeling as though rules have been broken or favoritism has occurred.

Some schools will actively ask you for information about your child to help them make teacher decisions (this is most common at the elementary level, relatively uncommon at the middle school level, and pretty much unheard of at the high school level). If that is the case, look at the phrases and descriptions in the appendix and see if they can help you describe your child in a way that is likely to produce a good match. And, if you have your heart set on Mrs. Peisner in the second grade, make sure that you are using language in your description that connects to Mrs. Peisner's teacher qualities (just try not to make it too glaringly obvious).

On the flip side, if there is a specific teacher that you do *not* want your child to have, then make sure to highlight in your letter the teacher qualities that do not work well with your child (which, coincidentally, happen to be the teacher qualities shared by the teacher you don't want).

If your school doesn't ask parents for information to help with the teacher selection process, go ahead and give it to them anyway. Write a letter or e-mail that discusses who your child is as a student and that describes the teacher qualities that you think will match well with your child. A couple tips about how to do this when the school doesn't already have a process in place:

- Start your letter with a polite explanation of why you are writing to the school. Look at the sample in the appendix for an idea of how to do this.
- Send the letter (or e-mail) to a guidance counselor and cc an administrator.
- Make sure you know when the teacher assignment process happens so that you don't send your letter too late or too early. It is likely that the process will happen late in the school year or during the summer for elementary and middle schools, and sometime in the spring or early summer for high schools. You can call the school to get this information; most likely a guidance counselor or the school secretary will know the timeline.
- Look for some sort of acknowledgment that your letter was received. If you have not heard anything back after several weeks, send a polite e-mail asking if the school received your note. You're not looking for any type of detailed response from the school, just a simple "Yes, thank you, we got your letter."

UNDERSTAND THE DIFFERENCES BETWEEN ELEMENTARY, MIDDLE, AND HIGH SCHOOLS

Most of this chapter is really geared toward elementary school parents. In elementary schools, students typically have just one teacher each year, and the teacher selection process is controlled entirely by the adults in the building (potentially the principal, but there could also be a teacher team that helps run the process). That means that the educators have almost complete control over deciding which students are going to be paired with which teachers.

Things are completely different for high schools. When building high school master schedules, teacher assignments are oftentimes done by a computer, not by a person. Students sign up for the courses they want, the principal decides which teachers are going to teach which courses, and then a software program figures out the best configuration of classes to make it all work. If your child gets a great sophomore English teacher, and her best friend gets a crummy sophomore English teacher, that was almost certainly the luck of the draw as the computer program played out, not a specific decision made by the principal.

That does not mean, however, that there is no flexibility in the system. Behind the scenes, there is the possibility of engineering some individual choices. There are situations in which a high school principal will make sure that a specific student doesn't end up with a specific teacher (usually because they had been in a class together previously and it didn't work out). High schools also have some discretion in shifting students from one section to another after the master schedule has been created. Here are a few points specifically for high school parents to consider (elementary and middle school parents can earmark this section and come back to it in a couple years):

- There is nothing wrong with providing a high school with information about your child to help them in making teacher matches, and the same general advice applies: know your child, know the teachers, and don't make specific requests. The school doesn't have the same discretion, however, in making specific assignments, so don't expect the same sort of results that you might hope for at the elementary level.
- If you want to provide a high school with information about your child to help with teacher selection, your best bet is to focus on one or two specific subjects. If there is a specific math teacher that you are hoping for, put your energies into describing your child's personality and learning needs in the context of math, as opposed to more generally. High schools have the most flexibility when looking at one or two specific subjects in the teacher assignment process.
- If your child is going to take a specialized class with only a couple teachers who teach it—say Advanced Placement Calculus—or your child is requesting a class with only a few teachers in the department—say an art class or a music class—there is more flexibility for the school to match students with teachers. There are typically a bazillion teachers teaching a bazillion sections of Freshman English, so specific assignments are likely not going to happen there. But if your child wants to take a photography

class and there are just two teachers teaching photography, you might be able to get your child into one specific teacher's section.
- Sometimes it's possible for your child to pick a specific teacher by picking a specific course. For example, imagine a popular business teacher who's the only teacher who teaches those courses. If a student took a previous course with him and really enjoyed it, then the student could sign up for more business courses knowing that this teacher would be the person teaching them. Especially as high school students get to their junior and senior years, they frequently have more flexibility in the courses that they want to take. There's nothing wrong with a student taking some courses specifically because they know that they are taught by an outstanding teacher.
- One thing that will probably not work is to make a specific teacher request after a master schedule has already been put together. It's not uncommon to have students and parents who request teacher changes during the summer or at the start of the school year. The goal might be to try to get into the same class as a friend, to get into a popular teacher's class, or to try to escape from a less-than-good teacher. In those cases, a high school principal is likely going to say "No." Allowing students to switch from teacher to teacher after-the-fact wreaks havoc on a high school master schedule, and schools probably won't allow it. Legitimate class changes are one thing—for example, if a course is simply too difficult and a student needs to move out of it—but high schools are unlikely to approve course changes because of teacher preference. If you want to help your child get a specific teacher, you need to do it prior to the teacher assignment process rather than afterward.

The focus so far has been on the teacher selection process for elementary schools and high schools, and the differences between the two. Middle schools are somewhere in-between and can vary tremendously. Smaller middle schools may have only one subject-specific teacher at each grade level, so there are no choices available. Other middle schools have assigned teacher "teams," meaning that an English teacher, math teacher, social studies teacher, and science teacher (and potentially a World Language teacher) are paired together to teach the same, common group of students. In those cases, you might have some flexibility in requesting one teacher team or the other, but you can't pick individual teachers who aren't part of that team.

Other middle schools (especially bigger ones) might use more of a high school model with assigning classes so that students could end up with a wide variety of teachers depending on how the course assignment software plays out.

The key for you as a parent is to know how your child's middle school assigns students to teachers and then work within that system. If the school has multiple teaching teams and you have heard great things about one of the teams, try to steer the school in that direction. If it's a big middle school and teacher assignments are handled like a high school, use the high school tips to your advantage. Either way, there's nothing wrong with contacting the school before teachers are assigned and giving them information about your child to help them in the selection process. Just make sure you are putting that information into the context of how the school assigns students and teachers. (If you're not sure what system the school uses, contact a guidance counselor—they are usually the best source of information on these topics.)

One final, Machiavellian note to end this chapter. The principal of the school knows who the good and the less good teachers are, and she needs to assign students to all of them. And the reality is that student assignment is a zero-sum game: every kid needs to get assigned, and every teacher needs to be teaching a pretty equivalent number of students.

What you want in this zero-sum game is to increase the likelihood that your child is going to get a good teacher "fit" so that he will have a good year. Your child may not end up getting Mrs. Peisner, the star second-grade teacher that all the parents rave about, but your child can still get someone who will complement your child's strengths and areas of need.

Now, some parents may feel guilty about this: they got a good teacher fit because they asked for it, but their neighbor's child got that teacher that nobody wants. Remember, that's not your problem to solve. If there's a teacher that no one wants, then it is the school's responsibility to help that teacher improve or to build a case that she needs to move out of the school. Your job is to advocate for your child. And if your child ends up not getting a good fit, then follow the advice in chapter 3 to make the year as good as possible nonetheless.

Chapter 3

How Do You Make the Best of an Average Teacher?

Imagine this scenario: A middle school parent, every time her son receives a grade lower than a B, sends an angry e-mail to the teacher, arguing about the grade and demanding to know what the teacher is going to do to improve it. The parent is convinced that all of her son's teachers are incompetent (which they probably aren't), that making as much noise as possible is the best way to address the situation (which it probably isn't), and that her child can do no wrong (which he probably can).

What's likely to happen? After receiving a few of this parent's e-mail rants, the child's teachers will start to tune out the substance of the parent's complaints. They will also become very careful with the way they interact with the child, concerned that any comment or action could be misconstrued when it's described at home.

And what's especially unfortunate in this all-too-common situation? The parent probably has some legitimately good feedback that, if the teachers were to consider it, could lead to a better educational experience for the child. But by creating such an antagonistic relationship with the teachers, and by crying wolf so often, the parent's nuggets of real truth and insight become lost in the overwhelming rubble of her complaints.

There are lots of fantastic teachers out there, but not everyone is a rock star. And that's okay. Your child won't have a great teacher (or great teachers) every year, but an "average" teacher will still help your child learn and succeed. When you suspect that your child is in a less-than-great classroom, please don't react the same way as the parent discussed previously. The key to supporting your child in a classroom that may not always be stellar is to:

- Build a good relationship with the teacher(s)
- Where and when possible, learn about the class curriculum
- Monitor your child's progress.

BUILD A GOOD RELATIONSHIP

Your child's teacher(s) will spend a huge amount of time with your child. In middle school and high school, each teacher will likely have direct contact with your child for anywhere from a couple hours to seven or eight hours a week (depending on your child's schedule). In elementary school, this is obviously magnified to the point where your child's teacher may very well spend more waking hours with your child than you do during the week. For someone who spends that much time with your child—and is responsible for helping your child learn and succeed—it is critically important to build a good relationship, for a couple different reasons.

First, a good relationship facilitates honest communication. If the teacher notices that your child is struggling academically, is having a bad day, or seems to be behaving in an unusual manner, you want the teacher to feel comfortable reaching out to you to share that information.

In addition, a good relationship allows you to communicate honestly with the teacher. Let's say your child thinks the teacher doesn't like him, feels lost in class, or is having a conflict with another student. If you have a good relationship with the teacher, it makes it that much easier for you to reach out to the teacher to help resolve the situation.

Finally (and this may sound a little Machiavellian, but it's true), if your child's teacher(s) like you, they are even more likely to treat your child in a positive manner. In a perfect world, teachers would always be nice to their students and it wouldn't matter what the students' parents were like. But the reality is that teachers are human just like everyone else, and if they think positively of you, that makes them even more inclined to treat your child positively.

So, a good relationship is important for many reasons. But how do you go about building a good relationship with a teacher? Here are a few tips:

- First impressions matter—First impressions tend to set the tone for a relationship, and you want a teacher's first impression of you to be positive. To accomplish that, the following are helpful:
  - After the first couple days of school, send a nice e-mail to your child's teacher(s). Keep it short and say something to the effect of, "I just wanted you to know how happy I am to have Samantha in your class this year. Please don't ever hesitate to contact us if you have a question or concern,

and best wishes for the start of the school year!" That message communicates positive support, makes sure the teacher has your preferred e-mail if she needs it, and sets a positive tone from the first encounter.
  - When you meet the teacher face-to-face for the first time, only speak in positive terms, smile a lot, and keep it short. Let the teacher know that you are happy to have your child in his class (even if you aren't), and try to positively mention something that your child is doing in class or has done in class ("James really enjoyed working on the solar system project").
  - Send an e-mail or hand-written note out of the blue to call positive attention to something in the class. For example, if your child did well on a spelling test, send the teacher a note and say something like "Robert was so proud of his grade on the spelling test—thank you for your work with him to help him be successful!" Don't overdo this—you shouldn't be sending the teacher a positive note every week—but the teacher will really appreciate a nice note that he or she wasn't expecting.
- Use a positive tone in all of your communications—After that first positive impression, make sure you maintain a positive tone in your communications going forward, even if you need to say something negative. Try to always start and finish your notes, e-mails, phone calls, or face-to-face conversations with a positive statement and make clear that any negative information is in the context of an overall positive experience.

LEARN ABOUT THE CURRICULUM

Building a good relationship with your child's teacher(s) is the first step in supporting your child in an "average" class. The next step is having a sense of the class curriculum.

One of the things about schooling that can stress parents out is that most parents don't really know what their kids *should* be learning. Parents might vaguely remember what they studied in first grade, or middle school, or chemistry, but hazy memories of one's own schooling are not the best points of comparison.

Parents certainly don't need to become curriculum experts, but especially if your child is in a less-than-stellar classroom, it's a good idea for you to be generally knowledgeable about the major skills and content that your kid should acquire. Here are some general tips to help you do that:

- Where to learn about the curriculum—The best place to look for a curriculum summary is on a district or school website, or on a teacher website or class syllabus. Many school districts create "pacing guides," which are summaries of what students should be learning and when they should be learning it. If your district does have curriculum pacing guides, they are a great place to start.

Some districts or schools even publish day-by-day lesson plans for individual subjects and grade levels, but it's probably not a good idea to follow them too closely: great teachers tend to adjust the curriculum based on student progress. Therefore, daily lesson plans (especially ones created in large districts) may not always accurately detail exactly what your child is doing on a given day. And remember, your goal isn't to become a curriculum expert, just to have a general sense of the big-picture curricular goals in your child's classroom(s).

- How to know what's important—At the elementary level, reading and math skills are especially important; they set the foundation for many of the concepts that kids will learn in middle and high school. But you should get nervous when a teacher or school seems to leave out the other subjects: science, social studies, the arts, physical education, and so on.

How well a child is able to read, and understand what he is reading, depends in large part on what is called "background knowledge," which is the set of interwoven facts and experiences that a story or text assumes a reader has. The other subjects, such as science, social studies, or physical education, are where students learn the background knowledge that helps them develop as early readers and thinkers. And, as students become older, those other subjects become increasingly important in their own right.

- Have curriculum conversations with teachers—Most schools will have scheduled times for parents to come in and have one-on-one conversations with teachers about their children (often called "parent-teacher conferences"). And any parent should be able to schedule a meeting with his child's teacher(s) if necessary. The key during these meetings is to come in with the right approach and to know the right questions to ask to help you learn about class curricula. Here are some tips:

The right mindset:
  - Treat the teacher as a curriculum expert who can help provide you with practical and useful information.
  - Ask lots of questions and listen carefully to the answers, potentially taking notes if that is helpful to you.
  - Anytime the teacher uses a term or concept that is unfamiliar to you, ask her to explain it.
  - Your goal is to have a general understanding of curricular goals, not a detailed one—don't sweat the individual points too much.
  - Ask the teacher to provide as many practical examples as possible of different learning goals and to connect those examples to samples of your child's work if available.

- Get the teacher's advice about where to go to learn more about classroom curricula.

Questions to ask:
- What are the main skills and knowledge that you want my child to master this year?
- Can you give me some practical examples of what that looks like?
- Can you show me in my child's work the extent to which she is acquiring those knowledge and skills?
- What are the areas where my child is ahead of expectations? What are the areas where my child is behind?
- What can I be doing at home to support her?
- Where can I go if I have questions about what my child should be learning?

MONITOR YOUR CHILD'S PROGRESS

Once you have a general sense of what your child should be learning, here is the next (and arguably bigger) question: Is my child actually learning those things?

Most parents will probably turn to report cards and grades to get a sense of their child's progress, and those are good places to start. But they should not be all you rely on. In a great teacher's class, grades will communicate really accurate and important information about how your child is doing. In a less-than-great classroom, however, grades can communicate different things. There are students who work their tails off but struggle to learn and end up earning Cs in the process. Then there are students who are superbright but frequently fail to do their work and end up earning Cs in the process. If you happen to be the parent of both types of students, how do you know what that "C" really means? Is your child behind where he should be academically but has a great work ethic, or has he learned most of what he should but has lazy work habits?

The following paragraphs provide advice on how you can go beyond grades to track your child's academic progress.

Look for patterns of feedback from the teacher—When your child brings home completed work—whether it's simple classwork, quizzes, tests, projects, papers, and so on—take some time to review the teacher's feedback and your child's level of success. Do you see any patterns? For example, does your child get consistently positive comments with few errors? Does your child tend to understand the concepts but make little mistakes?

One caveat: some parents expect that a teacher will provide lots of feedback on every piece of work, but that's not a realistic expectation. Teachers will likely put more time into more important assignments, so expect more feedback on the bigger tests, projects, or papers, and don't be surprised if a simple smiley face, sticker, or check-mark suffices for smaller examples of work.

Follow up with the teacher, when appropriate—If you see a concerning pattern of feedback from the teacher, follow up. Here's a real-life example to demonstrate how this might work: imagine that a child gets a series of comments from his teacher about work being turned in late. The parent reaches out to the teacher to understand what's happening, has a quick face-to-face conversation with the teacher to clarify, and the teacher's comments help the parent set up a new routine with the child to help him keep track of his assignments. The parent held off on reaching out to the teacher until she saw a real pattern that was concerning, and until it became clear that her son's behaviors were starting to hurt him academically. But once the parent realized something needed to be done, she relied on the teacher to help advise her on how to help her son.

Engage your child about her schoolwork—One of the things that parents learn is that it's really hard to find out about what actually happens to their children at school. The standard "How was school today?" questions are often met with a simple "Good," and there's only so much time in a busy day to catch up. So, parents have to ask more specific questions and really pay attention to those occasions when their kids decide to open up. These are three tricks to help learn about what your kids are learning:

- Ask specific questions: Rather than asking "How was school today?" ask more specific questions; for example, "What are two interesting facts that you learned in Science class today?" "Tell me something that you learned in school today that you think I don't already know." "What was the most boring thing your teacher talked about today?" By asking more specific questions you're more likely to get your child talking about her day and experiences, and in the process gain some insight into what is actually happening.
- Let your kids correct you: This might sound silly, but it really can work. If your child is studying the water cycle in class, say something that you know is wrong: "In the water cycle, isn't 'precipitation' when it gets really hot and water disappears from the ground up into the air?" Children typically love to correct their parents, and they will often bite the hook, proceeding to tell you all about how the water cycle works. If you play ignorant, they will love the chance to prove that they are smarter than you.
- Invite your kids to show off: Let's say your child is working on a presentation for her history class, but you know almost nothing about it. Go ahead and ask her if she wants to practice her presentation with you. If she takes

the bait, you're likely to get a deeper insight into what the class is doing and into how much your child is learning. Just like kids enjoy correcting their parents, they also enjoy the occasional opportunity to show off—when you can, give them the opportunity to do so.

Review standardized test scores—This piece of advice comes with some big caveats. Most states have annual standardized tests, usually starting in third grade and extending through high school, that are intended to provide information about how a student is progressing relative to state curricular standards. These tests vary in quality and rigor from state to state, and their purpose is not really to provide actionable information about individual students. In other words, a teacher or parent can't look at the results from these tests and say, "Johnny looks like he needs more help on these specific concepts." The purpose of the tests is more to provide a bird's-eye view of how students in a class, school, district, and state are doing.

That having been said, standardized tests can be somewhat useful for parents because they provide an outside, objective, and comparative look into your child's progress. Here is some brief advice on how to use standardized test scores to your advantage:

- Understand what the test is measuring and how it reports information—These tests typically report two useful pieces of information: how your child is doing compared to the state expectations and how your child is doing compared to other children. The first piece of information is usually expressed as an achievement level: proficient, advanced, developing, failing, and so on. These are broad categories that communicate whether or not your child is generally on track with the state expectations. The second piece of information is usually expressed as a percentile: 50th %, 30th %, 99th %, and so on. This tells you how your child's score compares with other students in the state at the same grade level.
- Look for similarities and differences between your child's score and other information—If your child earns good grades in school and scores highly on the state's standardized test, that's an extra piece of confirmation that your child is progressing well. If, however, the grades and standardized test scores don't align, that could indicate something. For example, if your child earns good grades in school but does poorly on standardized tests, you might want to dig a little deeper with your child's teacher(s) to understand the discrepancy. Conversely, if your child earns poor grades in school but does really well on standardized tests, you might want to look at your child's work habits and academic behaviors (without generalizing too much, this tends to be more of a boy phenomenon, in which a student might understand ideas quickly but not consistently complete homework or classwork).

- Don't put too much stock in one standardized test score—Here's a real-life example that occurred in a state that allowed students who didn't pass the standardized test the first time to take it one more time about a week later. A middle school student scored in the 35th percentile the first time he took the test, and then a week later scored in the 80th percentile on the retake. Did he magically learn tons of new information in the week between? Of course not: the difference was that he wasn't motivated the first time he took the test, and he was motivated the second time when he had to retake it. While this is an extreme example, it's pretty common for students' standardized test scores to vary 10–15 percentile points (or more) from one year to the next. So, take those scores with a grain of salt.
- Pay attention to patterns over time—If that middle schooler's parents in the story above had put too much stock in his first score, they would have thought he had learned very little, only to get a completely different impression with his second score. The key is to pay attention to trends over time. If your child consistently scores below the 30th percentile on standardized tests, that probably means that she is behind where the average student should be. One year with a bad test score is enough to raise interest, but multiple years of consistently low scores may very well indicate a real phenomenon to pay attention to. The reverse is also true: one good test score is certainly something to celebrate, but multiple years of high test scores suggest that your child is performing above expectations.

If you have big concerns, consider educational testing—If you see a continuing pattern of slow academic progress on the part of your child, and things don't seem to be getting better, you might want to ask your child's school about educational testing. You are free to go to a private psychologist to conduct your own testing at your own expense, and there can be benefits to that if you are in the financial situation to be able to do so, but the recommendation would be to start with your child's school system before going to outside experts.

Educational testing provides detailed, specific information about your child's intellectual abilities and achievement. School systems will typically only conduct educational testing when they believe a child may have some sort of underlying disability that is inhibiting his progress, and it is not recommended that parents pursue this route just because their child isn't reaching his potential, or seems to be below average in achievement. This is an avenue to pursue when your child is really struggling in school, and multiple attempts by the teacher(s) to address this over an extended period of time do not seem to be working.

Chapter 4

How Do You Work with a Teacher about a Question or Concern?

Let's say you are happy—or at least reasonably happy—with your child's teacher, but you have a concern or a question. Maybe your child is struggling under a mountain of homework that feels excessive, maybe your child doesn't seem to be making much progress with her reading skills, or maybe the teacher always seems to be behind in her grading.

It isn't as though things have gone horribly wrong, but this question or concern is important enough that you want to do something about it. So, what do you do?

There's nothing wrong with contacting a teacher and asking a question or expressing a concern. But there are effective and ineffective ways to do that. When asking a question or communicating a concern to your child's teacher:

- Be polite
- Seek to understand
- Be clear and specific
- Use e-mail carefully
- Don't get your child involved
- Pick your battles
- Involve administration as a last resort.

BE POLITE

Unfortunately, some parents can be great to talk to face-to-face but come across as real jerks online. E-mail exchanges that frequently include snide comments or use a lot of sarcasm will end up offending teachers and give a parent a negative reputation. This can then put a kid at a disadvantage because teachers tended to be wary of the parent, always worried that they will do or say something that could lead to a nasty note.

There's an old adage that one hears frequently in the South: you catch more flies with honey than you do with vinegar. When parents approach situations with a polite tone, they get to better solutions for their kids and avoid making enemies in the process.

It's completely understandable that parents get emotional when it comes to their kids, but that doesn't excuse a lack of basic manners. Even when you're frustrated or angry, please stay polite in your interactions with school staff. It is ultimately better strategically, and it's just common courtesy.

SEEK TO UNDERSTAND

There is a chapter in Stephen Covey's famous book *The Seven Habits of Highly Effective People* called "Seek First to Understand," and the chapter focuses on the importance in any interaction of trying to understand the perspectives of others. That's an important message to internalize. When seated across from someone who's frustrated, angry, or upset, it's all too easy to react *against* the emotions and words being expressed. But when, instead of reacting against them, one takes the time to try to understand the other person's perspective, it typically leads to much better outcomes.

Most people's behavior makes perfect sense to them. If your child's teacher is acting in a way that doesn't make sense to you, seek first to understand the reason behind the teacher's behavior before judging or criticizing it. You may end up not agreeing with the reason, but a huge percentage of frustrations between parents and teachers can arise from some sort of misunderstanding. And those misunderstandings could have been avoided by an attempt to understand the other person's perspective, rather than beginning a conversation or interaction with assumptions or preconceptions.

One other important point to keep in mind when forming an opinion about your child's teacher is that your primary source of information about the teacher is most likely your child, and that's problematic. Children of all ages are notoriously poor reporters of objective reality. They tend to see the world through their own specific lens, and they can also be very strategic in what they choose to report (or choose not to report). Here's a great piece of advice that a kindergarten teacher liked to give to parents on the back-to-school night at the start of every year: "If you promise to only believe half of what your kids tell you about me, I promise to only believe half of what they tell me about you."

Please listen to your children's stories about school and teachers and take them seriously. But please also take your children's stories with a decently sized grain of salt.

BE CLEAR AND SPECIFIC

In general, most parents want to avoid conflict with their children's teachers. They want to be respectful, and they don't want the teacher to form a negative impression of them or their child. And so, when they have a concern or a question, they can be circumspect when trying to describe it, framing the concern in vague or general terms. Rather than saying "Johnny thinks you don't like him because of comments that he says you make to him," they make general statements like "I was wondering if it would be helpful if you were to adopt a more supportive approach with the students in class."

Vague statements typically leave a teacher scratching her head, trying to read between the lines and potentially getting defensive. Make sure you are clear about the specific question or concern and try to stick to how it specifically affects your child. Just use polite language when doing so.

USE E-MAIL CAREFULLY

Educators both love and hate e-mail. On the one hand, it allows them to quickly and efficiently communicate with people. On the other hand, it's easy to become inundated with e-mails and for an e-mail conversation to go astray. Here are a couple rules to help parents use e-mail effectively when communicating with a school:

- Keep your tone consistently polite—At this point, this piece of advice may be sounding like a broken record, but it's hard to emphasize too much how important it is to be polite. When you write a teacher (or administrator) an e-mail, read it before you hit "Send." If it sounds impolite or judgmental, rewrite it.
- If it requires a long answer, don't do it by e-mail—E-mail is great for quick queries: Does Jared need to pack a lunch for the field trip on Friday? Is there an afternoon next week when we could set up a meeting? But if you're looking for lots of information or an answer to a complicated question, avoid relying on e-mail; instead, schedule a phone call or meeting.

- Remember that teachers have limited time for e-mail—Elementary school teachers typically have between twenty and thirty students in their classes, and middle and high school teachers can have over one hundred students that they see each day (and some teachers, especially physical education teachers, can easily have many hundreds of students that they work with each week). If the parents of each of those students send regular e-mails to the teacher, then there's no time left for teaching. Please be respectful of the fact that most of a teacher's time is spent teaching, planning lessons, creating and grading assessments, meeting with colleagues, handling administrative paperwork, and so on. If you find that you're sending your child's teacher daily e-mails, you're probably overdoing it (unless a specific plan has been put in place that calls for daily communication).
- After two e-mails back and forth, switch to a phone call or a face-to-face conversation—It's not uncommon for an e-mail string to begin innocuously enough, but then, after a couple messages back and forth, to start to get nasty. The thing is, e-mails lack the tone and body language of an in-person conversation, and it's easy for words or sentiments to be misconstrued. If you and a teacher have already traded two messages back and forth and the situation isn't resolved, figure out a time to talk by phone or face-to-face. Don't let yourselves get dragged into a nitpicky e-mail battle that will leave both of you angry or frustrated.

DON'T GET YOUR CHILD INVOLVED

If you do have a concern that you need to discuss with a teacher, try not to talk about it openly with your child. While most parents try to follow this rule, parents can sometimes fall into the trap of openly criticizing a teacher at home in front of their child. Or even worse, bring a child with them to school to engage in a negative conversation with a teacher.

The problem with this is twofold. First, it means that the child may lose respect for the teacher, damaging that relationship. Second, it means that the child could feel empowered to ignore the teacher's directions and rules, potentially leading to classroom confrontations.

Whatever you may privately think of a teacher (or any school staff member), please keep those concerns from your child. That doesn't mean that you shouldn't do anything about the concerns, far from it. But adults need to be able to have adult conversations without children being dragged in unless absolutely necessary.

PICK YOUR BATTLES

Here's another real-life story in which a parent gets incensed about the librarian at his son's elementary school. His son, who is only in second grade but is an advanced reader, goes to the school library hoping to check out a specific book. But the librarian tells the student that he can't check out the book because it's reserved for older children. This drives the parent crazy: "If my son is able to read a more advanced book, then he should be able to check it out! It's ridiculous that certain books are reserved for older children. I'm going to get in touch with the principal and get her to change the rule!"

While the parent's frustration is understandable, this is *not* a battle worth fighting. Schools are trying to meet the needs of all their students while also dealing with the reality of finite resources, and that means that they have to make rules that prioritize different students at different times. At the end of the day, maybe the librarian's rule is a bad rule, but it's just not important enough to do something about. You may not always agree with a teacher's or a school's practices, but make sure you save your energy for the issues that really matter.

INVOLVE ADMINISTRATION AS A LAST RESORT

When a parent contacts a principal with a classroom concern, chances are the principal will ask the parent to first reach out to the teacher. As a general rule, questions or concerns can best be resolved by the people directly involved.

But there are times when a concern is important enough to bring directly to the administration. If you believe your child is being physically or emotionally harmed by a school staff member; if you have attempted to resolve a situation with a teacher and have been unsuccessful; or if you are concerned that a classroom or schoolwide practice is actively damaging children's education, then you should contact an administrator directly. After listening to your concern, the administrator may not necessarily agree with your perspective or take the action you would like her to, but administrators need to know about more serious parent concerns.

And if you are on the fence about what to do, go ahead and reach out to an administrator. If nothing else, they can provide some perspective and advice even if they do not take immediate action.

Chapter 5

How Do You Handle a Truly Bad Teacher?

So far in the book, the focus has been on good teachers and average teachers. But it is time to shift to the opposite end of the spectrum. Unfortunately, there is a real possibility that your child may have an ineffective teacher at some point, and knowing how to handle it is critical.

This chapter begins with a peek behind the K–12 personnel curtain. The human resource practices in the business and education worlds can be quite different, and these differences can be confusing and frustrating for parents used to working in private industry. For that reason, the chapter starts with a summary of how hiring, supervision, and firing work in public schools. At the same time, there's an important secret to know: parents can be one of a principal's greatest resources in removing ineffective teachers. But parents have to understand the system to help make the system work.

After learning about the human resource system, the chapter looks at what parents should do when their child has a truly lousy teacher, both in terms of addressing the teacher and in terms of mitigating the educational damage to your child. A bad class, or even a bad year, is not an insurmountable challenge. But it can take some effort on a parent's part to overcome the effects of an ineffective teacher.

PERSONNEL PRACTICES IN PUBLIC EDUCATION: THE GOOD, THE BAD, AND THE UGLY

If you read the "traits of an effective teacher" vignettes in the appendix, you learned about Sue. Unfortunately, Sue was an example of an ineffective teacher. The following real-life meeting happened when a parent met with the school's principal to share concerns about Sue.

Prior to this meeting, the parent had already tried all of the typical avenues to address the issues—he had traded e-mails with Sue with polite questions, met with her to discuss the concerns, and held his son accountable at home for low grades in the class. But the parent had reached his limit, and he didn't know what to do other than meet with the principal.

In the meeting, the parent and the principal were sitting in a conference room, and the parent reviewed his long list of concerns. The principal sat and listened politely until the parent finally asked, "So, why is it that this teacher still has her job? She is clearly incompetent, you haven't disagreed with a thing I've said, and this has been going on now for months. Can you please promise me that you will be firing her tomorrow?"

The principal just shook her head politely and replied, "I'm going to pretend you didn't just ask me a personnel question about a specific teacher, because I can't discuss specific personnel issues with a parent. Instead, I am going to assume that you asked me a more general question about teacher supervision and evaluation, and what it takes for a teacher to lose his or her job because of low performance. That I am completely comfortable discussing."

Here's the explanation the principal gave to the parent.

Tenured and Nontenured Teachers

There are generally two categories of teachers: nontenured teachers and tenured teachers. In some states or districts, they may use different terms—teachers with professional status, teachers with continuing contracts—but it all boils down to the difference between having tenure and not having tenure.

If a teacher does not have tenure, then she can typically be removed from her position within a given year, but there is a process that has to be followed and there is a fair amount of documentation needed. A principal cannot usually fire a nontenured teacher without showing some sort of cause, but the threshold for what constitutes "cause" is much lower.

For a tenured teacher, it is typically a two-year minimum process to remove someone. Unless they do something totally egregious—hit a student, sleep with a student, steal money from the district, create a meth lab in their classroom—most tenured teachers have at least a two-year minimum period before they have to worry about losing their jobs. And the paperwork and time required on a principal's part to get to that point are substantial.

Documenting Poor Performance

In order for a teacher to lose her job, a principal needs to document a pattern of ineffective behavior over time. And the teacher needs to be given multiple chances to improve. Depending on the human resource rules in effect (and these are typically set at the state and/or district level), principals can collect a variety of data about teacher performance—student achievement scores, parent feedback, and feedback from colleagues—but the primary type of performance documentation is classroom observations, similar to the observations of Sue and John that are described in the appendix.

An administrator will typically conduct at least a couple of formal observations in a teacher's classroom each year, depending on the approved process. In some districts or states, a principal can conduct as many formal observations of a teacher as he wishes each year; in other districts or states, a principal may only be able to conduct formal classroom observations of a tenured teacher once or twice every couple years.

If those observations document a pattern of ineffective performance, then a teacher can be put on what is typically called an "Improvement Plan." This Improvement Plan will have goals for the teacher to meet and can last anywhere from multiple months to a year. If the teacher meets the goals, then *poof*—the Improvement Plan goes away and the teacher is back to square one. If the teacher doesn't meet the goals of the Improvement Plan, then a principal begins to have a case for termination. But, depending on the labor laws in the state and the details of the employment contract, teachers can sometimes maintain their jobs for years even after a substantial amount of documentation has been collected.[1]

At this point in the meeting, the father turned to the principal with a resigned look on his face. "So, you're telling me that there is nothing I can do. My son has to endure a horrible teacher for the rest of the year, and all you can do, the principal of the school, is shake your head in commiseration?"

Fortunately, the principal had a better answer to that question. "No, there is something you can do as a parent." And that answer leads us to the next section.

WHAT PARENTS CAN DO ABOUT INEFFECTIVE TEACHERS

There are two broad categories of parental action when it comes to a bad teacher. On one side, parents can help to identify and put pressure on bad teachers, either leading to their ultimate improvement or dismissal. More important, however, are the steps that parents can take to limit their children's educational damage.

It's important, however, to make one critically important point before going any further. Throughout this book, there is an emphasis on the ways in which parents can work effectively, positively, and productively with teachers and administrators to achieve great things for their kids. The advice that follows is specifically focused on actions to take when those attempts have repeatedly failed, and a parent is concerned that a teacher is simply not doing his job.

So, when you are unfortunately at the point where you believe your child may have a truly lousy teacher and you want to do something about it, you need to:

- Follow a clear process of communication and documentation
- Stay focused on the core concern(s)
- Look for solutions, not vengeance
- Supplement your child's education outside of school, to the extent possible

Follow a Clear Process of Communication and Documentation

The concerns and communications that a parent has about a class should start at the parent-teacher level (and hopefully be resolved there). Despite this, some parents are quick to go nuclear when something goes wrong, even though doing so is usually neither effective nor appreciated. Here's a real-life, extreme example of what to avoid.

A middle school principal receives an e-mail over the weekend from the parent of a sixth grader at his school. The e-mail isn't actually addressed to the principal; he's just ccd on the message: the e-mail was addressed to (and again, this is a real-life example) the governor of the state. The e-mail also includes the district superintendent and the head of the school committee. The text of the e-mail says: "My daughter came home Friday night in tears. She tried out for the school play and did not get a part, and now she is completely distraught. I want to know why you allow schools to treat children this way, and I want to know what you are going to do about this situation!"

This is the first the principal has heard of the parent's complaint, and since he isn't the person to whom the e-mail was sent, he figures he can wait until the governor has had a chance to weigh in.

After several days of no response, the parent sends another angry e-mail asking why he's being ignored. At that point the principal figures he should probably reach out, so he gives the parent a call. The principal explains to the parent that there are only so many roles available for students, and those roles tend to go to the older kids who try out. But the principal would be happy to put the parent in touch with the teacher who directs the play. When that teacher calls the father, she explains that any student that doesn't get a role but still wants to participate in the play is welcome to help out with props, costumes, and makeup. The father is happy to hear about these other options and leaves the conversation reassured that everything will be okay.

That father handled the situation exactly the wrong way. Had he started by just reaching out to the teacher directing the play—or even e-mailing the principal and asking him who was in charge—he would have gotten a quicker solution without all of the drama (no pun intended).

When you are concerned that your child has a truly bad teacher, and you believe you may end up needing to speak with an administrator about the situation, there is a common communication process that you should follow (the exception would be when you have an immediate and serious concern about your child's physical or social-emotional safety, in which case you should jump straight to contacting an administrator). The process is as follows:

1. Write a friendly note to the teacher with specific questions and, if appropriate, requests.
2. If the first step doesn't work, then request a face-to-face conference with the teacher.
3. After the conference, send a follow-up e-mail to the teacher that summarizes the conversation and next steps.
4. If the problem still hasn't been solved, write a friendly note to an administrator and summarize the steps already taken.
5. If the problem continues, request a face-to-face conference with an administrator.
6. After that conference, send a follow-up e-mail to the administrator that summarizes the conversation and next steps.

When you do contact or meet with an administrator, chances are she will ask, "Have you already spoken with the teacher about this?" Your answer is then, "Yes, and here is a copy of that correspondence." Furthermore, because the administrator's next question is likely to be "And what happened as a result of that meeting?" you have notes and follow-up e-mails to indicate the steps that occurred, or did not occur, after you met with the teacher.

This will sound cold-hearted, but by following this process and creating documentation, you have accomplished two things. First, you have forced the teacher to acknowledge and address your concerns. Truly lousy teachers will try to avoid making any promises to a parent or putting themselves on the hook for any extra work. They will try to cloud the situation by speaking in vague terms or minimizing what occurred, especially when they are defending themselves to their boss. But by following and documenting the process, a parent creates clear evidence that prevents a lousy teacher from wiggling out of the situation.

Second, following the process and creating documentation gives an administrator evidence that can be used in the teacher's evaluation. When building a case to discipline or terminate a lousy teacher, an administrator needs to be able to point to specific documentation. A parent who hands a principal a pile of e-mail exchanges that document an ongoing issue that was not addressed, or in which a teacher agreed to take steps that he never took, is providing the principal with evidence that can be used to try to change a teacher's behavior, and potentially move that teacher out of the school.

Stay Focused on the Core Concern(s)

Whatever the concern may be—consistently being late returning graded work, using abusive language with students, a poor grasp of their subject matter, ineffective teaching practices—lousy teachers don't want to talk about it. In fact, they want to talk about practically anything else. So, when they get a message from a parent expressing a concern, they will try to change the topic. They might point out that the child has been a discipline problem in class. They might mention how they have been having health issues recently. They might take offense at the tone expressed in the parent's e-mail. They will do anything they can to shift the conversation away from the real underlying issue.

Don't let them.

Whatever your concern is, you have to stay laser-focused on it and not allow yourself to be distracted. If the teacher is outraged at the tone of your e-mail, apologize and return to the concern. If the teacher mentions her health problems, sympathize and then return to the concern. If the teacher tells you your son is having a behavior problem in class, let her know you will be holding your child accountable at home for his behavior and then return to the concern.

If you allow the conversation to stray from the core concern and get muddied up with extraneous stuff, you reduce the chances of getting a desired outcome. To help you stay focused on the core concern, here are four common "don't"s to avoid:

- Don't allow your emotions to take over—As frustrated, angry, or disappointed as you might be with a teacher, keep your emotions in check, whether in a face-to-face meeting or written correspondence, because they won't help the situation. In fact, they may undermine what you are trying to accomplish. Anger and bravado can sometimes intimidate a teacher and cause her to give in to a parent's wishes, but teachers are far more likely to dig in their heels and disregard a parent who comes off as aggressive or offensive.
- Don't let sympathy keep you from advocating for your child—Lousy teachers almost always have an excuse. But for every lousy teacher who

complains of health problems, financial problems, or challenges in their marriage, there are a dozen excellent teachers facing the same challenges who still show up every day and do their jobs well. There is nothing wrong with listening sympathetically to a teacher who is going through a tough time, and it's perfectly reasonable to cut a teacher some slack if their personal life is difficult. But after a certain point, reasonable requests for flexibility become an excuse for not doing one's job.

If a lousy teacher keeps providing you with excuses, show sympathy. But make sure you leave the meeting with a specific plan in place, and make sure your follow-up e-mail details what that plan will be. Sympathy for your child's teacher is no excuse for a substandard education for your child.

- Don't bring up undocumented perceptions or hearsay—School administrators frequently have parents tell me that "Everyone knows" that something is true, or that there are "Dozens of parents" who hold the same opinion that they do. Parents oftentimes use these sorts of assertions to bolster their arguments, to try to convince a teacher or administrator to take a certain course of action. For most administrators, however, it usually has the opposite effect.

When you communicate or meet with a teacher or administrator, stick to the facts of your child's situation, focusing especially on facts that are independently verifiable. For example, if a teacher has not handed back any graded work for over a month, that is a verifiable fact. Be very careful when you mention your child's perceptions about the teacher—rather than saying "You are always giving my daughter dirty looks," say instead "My daughter tells me that you look at her in a mean way; whether true or not, that is her perception"—and never mention what you may have heard other parents or children say about the teacher. If you do bring up perceptions or hearsay, it allows the teacher to dispute those statements and then turn the discussion into a "he said, she said" argument that strays from the real concerns.

One additional piece of advice connected to this topic: When parents tell an administrator, "Lots of other parents have the same concern," the standard answer will likely be "Well, please have them contact me separately." More often than not, the administrator will never hear from any other parents. But on some occasions, they might and that pattern of independent correspondence from multiple parents puts the administrator in a better position to deal with the teacher. So, if you hear from other parents who have the same concern that you do, encourage them to take the same steps that you are by contacting the teacher and, if necessary, contacting administration.

Look for Solutions, Not Vengeance

Dealing with an ineffective teacher can be incredibly frustrating. You know that this person is inhibiting your child's academic progress, and it can feel as though you are powerless to prevent it.

Some parents take a teacher's incompetence personally, especially if they believe that a teacher is being mean to their child. As a result, these parents may want vengeance: if this adult is hurting their child's education, then they will hurt the teacher's job.

As emotionally gratifying as it might feel to take out your frustration on an incompetent teacher, don't do it. Your job is not to discipline a teacher, your job as a parent is to find a solution for your child. If a teacher perceives that a parent is "after" him, then he can try to distract from his incompetence by arguing that a parent is making personal attacks. Let school administration handle the personnel implications; you need to put aside your personal frustrations about the teacher and situation and search for an outcome that addresses your underlying concerns.

In the following pages, there are some semi-common solutions that either you could propose or that the school might propose to you.

Change the teacher—To a parent, this can seem like the most straightforward and preferable solution: if the teacher is incompetent, give my child a different teacher. For the school, however, this can be problematic. At the elementary level, principals are trying to keep class sizes balanced; at the middle school level, there may just be one subject-specific teacher for the grade level or teacher team; and at the high school level, changing one teacher can have a cascading effect on a student's overall schedule. In addition, you may not be the only one hoping to move out of an incompetent teacher's class, and if the principal lets your child move, then chances are she will have a line of parents at the door the next day asking, "Well, if that parent's child can move, why can't mine?"

That doesn't mean that a teacher change is impossible. Principals do sometimes change students from one teacher to another based on a parent's request, but there needs to be a really good justification to do it. So, if you want to push for a teacher change, make it as palatable as possible for the principal. Describe what makes your situation unique so that a principal could justify moving your child but not another. Make sure you've followed a clear process before requesting a change. Show that you've tried multiple other options before making the request. Especially, if you can frame a change in terms that are not directly related to the teacher's quality, you make it that much easier for a principal to approve it.

And one final piece of advice: if you're able to get a principal to change your child's teacher, keep it to yourself. Because if you're able to get the principal to change your child's teacher and you then blab about it to other parents, you just made that helpful principal's life much more difficult.

Look at supplemental educational options—Assuming a teacher change is not an option, or as an intermediate step prior to requesting a teacher change, the school could take steps to supplement your child's educational experiences.

Some options could be tutoring with a separate teacher after or before school, supplemental educational opportunities online, or some sort of educational support plan. Tutoring with a different (and more competent) teacher is relatively easy for a school to arrange, and online educational opportunities are becoming more and more common. Free websites such as Khan Academy provide a range of curricular materials, and the school could create a plan for a separate educator to oversee your child's work with online curricula to supplement the class experience.

Parents will sometimes request out-of-school tutoring provided at the school's expense, but don't hold your breath on that: it's pretty uncommon and something schools really resist doing.

The last option, an educational support plan, would be most appropriate if your child is noticeably behind in her academic achievement (but not identified for special education supports) or noticeably advanced (but not part of an identified accelerated academic program). There is no simple or common template for this sort of thing, but schools certainly have the flexibility and ability to create individualized plans for students in unique circumstances, especially if that circumstance involves an incompetent teacher.

Creative alternatives—If you are at the point where you are fed up with a teacher and you are meeting with an administrator about the situation, ask him if there are any creative options available. There may not be, but by showing a willingness to consider creative solutions, you may prompt the administrator to consider nonconventional possibilities. Two quick real-life examples of this sort of flexibility: asking the principal to write a "support" letter to accompany a student's high school transcript that indicates that a class drop (which may be shown on the transcript) was not the academic fault of the student and enrolling students in online courses—both in middle school and in high school—in lieu of having them work with a less-than-competent teacher.

As a final footnote, here's one piece of "don't" advice: don't ask for something that your child doesn't deserve. Sometimes parents will make a complaint about a teacher and then use that complaint to try to gain something. It might just be an improved grade, but it doesn't always stop there. Essentially, parents in this situation are trying to create a sense of being "owed" by the school, and then cash in on that obligation in a way that isn't really appropriate. Please make sure that any requests you make are reasonable and directly relate to the substance of your concern. And please understand that your child's school will almost certainly not provide your child with some sort of advantage or privilege that wouldn't be provided to other students in the same situation.

Where Possible, Supplement Your Child's Education Outside of School

If your child has a truly lousy teacher, your biggest concern will likely be the longer-term effects on your child's academic progress. A year with a bad teacher can feel like a lost year, and many parents are concerned that the negative effects will mean their child will be behind for the next grade level or course.

In addition to the aforementioned possible steps that the school can be taking to supplement your child's education, there are things that you can do outside of school. The following tips can help you make sure that your child continues learning, even if a big chunk of that learning happens outside of school hours.

Have your child read as much as possible—Kids who read a lot will learn things despite a teacher's incompetence. What your child reads is less important than making sure that she does read, so it's strongly recommended that you find texts that your child enjoys. These could be comic books, magazines, novels, biographies, newspapers, and so on. Your child's ability to read improves with practice: the more your child reads at home, the more she is building her vocabulary (which is super important) and the more she is practicing and automatizing the mental mechanics of the reading process.

Read to your child—This is a great way to expose your child to more complicated texts, to help your child build his vocabulary, to model the importance of reading, and to have some quality family time. As one example, when your children are younger, read a book with them for fifteen minutes before they fell asleep. Then, when they get older, turn this routine into side-by-side reading: sitting side-by-side on the couch, read your own book while they read their own book before going to bed.

Create structured academic time—Some kids are naturally organized and they are able to manage their schoolwork relatively independently (gender bias alert: girls tend to be naturally better at this on average than boys). But many kids struggle to keep track of their assignments and schedules. This is especially true when children transition to middle and high school and they have to juggle multiple classes and different expectations from different teachers.

A good teacher helps students improve their organization skills, but a bad teacher can exacerbate the problems of a disorganized kid. You can help your child by building structured academic time into the day from an early age. This means identifying the specific time in the afternoon or evening, that is, time solely spent on academics: completing homework, studying for upcoming quizzes or tests, working on projects, and so on.

It's also a good idea to have a specific place where your child spends this academic time and have that space be free of distractions—for example, no music, no screens unless specifically part of the assignment, and no phone. Where possible, this place should not be your child's bedroom. The idea is that this time and place is just for schoolwork. And if your child insists that she is all done with her work (which may or may not be true), then use that time for independent reading. If your child learns that she can't negotiate her way into using the time differently, then she is more likely to go ahead and use the time well. By setting up this structured academic time, you both help your child stay on top of her schoolwork and you build behaviors that are more likely to continue in the future.

Build academic-ish activities into family time—This might sound more formal and complicated than it needs to be—the idea is simply to engage your child in activities with an academic bent but to not push things too far. Board games and card games that require strategy or math are easy ways to practice academic skills. Basically, if your child is counting spaces, counting money, remembering patterns, or plotting a strategy, then he is practicing skills that will help in school, even if he has a lousy teacher.

Create family cultural excursions—This one depends both on your family's available free time and financial resources, but there is interesting research that suggests that time spent on cultural activities—such as visiting a museum or attending a play—can reap academic benefits.[2] As was mentioned earlier in this chapter, reading skills are incredibly important in school, but reading ability is impacted by a student's background knowledge: that is, the information they already know about a topic. Cultural activities help to build background knowledge that supports reading and help to enrich topics that students are learning about. It's one thing to read a story about an elephant if you've never actually seen one; it is another thing entirely when you were at the zoo over the weekend and saw an elephant first-hand.

In addition to the benefits in supporting reading, cultural excursions also expand your child's general knowledge and appreciation for the world, can spark different areas of interest, and can be just plain fun for them and for you. More densely populated areas of the country are likely to offer more readily available, traditional cultural opportunities, but "culture" should be a broad term. Any excursions that help your child learn about his community, history, and the way the world works are valuable. They don't have to take place in a big museum or concert hall; they could just as easily take place on a farm or at a small-town fair.

Enlist professional help—If you are especially concerned about your child's academic progress in a lousy classroom, you can turn to private tutors or private organizational institutions. Professional help can be quite expensive, so it's recommended to explore support services offered by your child's school before turning to outside help, but ultimately you need to make the decisions that you think are in your child's best interests.

- Private tutors—It is not unheard of for elementary school students to use tutors, especially in the later grades, but professional tutors tend to be more prevalent for middle and high school students. If you are considering hiring a private tutor for your child, it's recommended that you seek out someone who either teaches or has taught the subject and/or grade level that is the subject of the tutoring. Current or former teachers are likely to understand both the subject area and how to teach it, and they are likely to be familiar with the specific academic expectations of your child's class or grade level. Your child's school may be able to recommend reputable tutors whom you could contact, and other parents can be a good source of information about their experiences with different tutors.
- Private professional organizations—These tend to fall into three categories: supplemental academics, remedial academics, and extra-academic. Supplemental academic organizations provide services beyond what one might receive in a public school; for example, advanced math classes, intensive art training, foreign language instruction, and so on. They are intended to enhance your child's education, not make up for a deficit.

In contrast, remedial academic organizations try to help your child improve with academic skills or knowledge that they should be learning in their school. These businesses are essentially organizational tutors, often with specific assessments, tools, and methods to help your child.

Finally, there are extra-academic organizations, which are not focused so much on specific academic skills but rather on supporting your child's social-emotional development, academic orientation, and organizational skills. These types of organizations might pair a child with adult mentors or arrange internship-type experiences.

One big recommendation is to make sure you research these organizations and speak to other parents about them before giving them your money. Some parents have very positive experiences with these types of supports, but it's important to find an organization that is reputable and that will be a good "fit" for your child's needs.

One final note about Sue before concluding this chapter. Sue was a real person, and she eventually did lose her job as a result of her incompetence.

And it was feedback from parents that helped build a case that it was simply time for her to go.

Those sorts of situations are hard to go through for everyone involved. At the same time, however, the Sues of the world are not paid to occupy space; they are paid to do a job. In many ways, the incompetence of people like Sue is a slap in the face to all of the wonderful teachers who work so hard, day in and day out.

Most importantly, the Sues of the world have a real detrimental impact on the educational lives of their students. When people like Sue are moved out of their jobs, it creates better educational opportunities for future kids who don't have to sit in their classes. And it's the efforts of concerned parents that can help to identify and document the incompetence of people like Sue. Most parents probably don't want to be the cause of someone losing their job—they just want to make sure their child gets the best education possible—but parental action can be a powerful force in identifying and documenting the incompetence of lousy teachers.

NOTES

1. A seminal article about this topic came out in the *New Yorker* back in 2009. Called "The Rubber Room," the article detailed how New York City teachers who had been rated as incompetent or charged with inappropriate actions continued to be employed but were taken out of schools and reassigned to empty rooms with no students. They essentially got paid to sit around and do nothing all day because the employment contract created so many bureaucratic rules to them being fired. The article is available at https://www.newyorker.com/magazine/2009/08/31/the-rubber-room.

2. Researcher Jay Greene has done a number of studies in this area. For a summary of one of his most compelling studies, with links to a number of other studies, you can read his article "An unexpectedly positive result from arts-focused field trips" published by The Brookings Institution. The article is available at https://www.brookings.edu/blog/brown-center-chalkboard/2018/02/16/an-unexpectedly-positive-result-from-arts-focused-field-trips-in-school/.

Section 2

STUDENT DISCIPLINE

WHY THE SCHOOL BUS IS LIKE *LORD OF THE FLIES*

This section's title was inspired by a conversation with an old friend.

He was reminiscing about his time back in middle school, remembering one boy in particular who used to terrorize the other kids on the bus: make fun of them, knock over their bags, threaten to get off at their stop and beat them up, and so on. At the time the other students did what they could to avoid the boy's attention, but they didn't see it as a particularly big deal. To a middle school mind, it seemed that that's just how kids were.

But now this friend's oldest son was in school himself, and was bringing home his own tales from the bus. His son also seemed to roll with things, accepting that that's what life is like for a kid in school. But for his father, this was a point of real concern. What if another kid picked on his son? Should he pass on the stories he was hearing to the school? What should he do about it?

That's when he posed the question that led to this section's title: "You know, the school bus really is like *Lord of the Flies*, isn't it?"

He was referring to the 1954 novel by William Golding (now a staple in middle and high school English classes) that follows a group of boys who are marooned on a deserted island. Over the course of the book, the boys become increasingly antagonistic toward each other, with the whole situation eventually devolving into murderous chaos.

What he meant with this comment was that, left to their own devices, kids can get out of control. They can be mean, petty, aggressive, and cruel.

The unfortunate response to his question is, "Yes, it really can be." And the negative behavior that happens on school buses can also happen in schools. The simple fact is, when you throw a bunch of kids of any age together, some of them are going to behave in ways they shouldn't.

This section is about student discipline: how schools try to manage student behavior, and what parents can do to support their children in the process.

The first two chapters focus on disciplinary nuts and bolts. Chapter 6 looks at the disciplinary "playbook" that administrators use: how they conduct investigations, and how they communicate with parents in the process. Chapter 7 focuses on disciplinary consequences, providing examples and discussing the impact of discipline on students' educational records. If you are interested in knowing about disciplinary minutiae, those two chapters are recommended reading.

If, however, you are less interested in getting into the weeds and more interested in looking at how disciplinary processes are likely to affect your child, then you can jump straight to chapters 8 and 9. Chapter 8 assumes that your child has gotten into trouble with his teacher, and walks you through how to handle it. Chapter 9 then focuses on more significant disciplinary situations that assume your child is in trouble with a school administrator. There may be concepts and advice in these chapters that refer back to the earlier, nut-and-bolts information from chapters 6 and 7. When that happens, you will be guided back to the pertinent places in earlier chapters.

Finally, chapter 10 is focused on helping you handle situations in which your child might be the victim of someone else's behavior. Again, when information from earlier chapters is incorporated, those pertinent spots will be pointed out.

Chapter 6

How Do Schools Deal with Student Discipline?

This chapter will help you understand how administrators deal with disciplinary situations. If your child gets into trouble, it is critical for you to understand the playbook that administrators are using to make their decisions. The main topics will be the parts of a disciplinary investigation (which covers things like due process and search and seizure) and how communication should work with parents during a disciplinary investigation.

In order to give you a concrete way to think about these concepts, however, the chapter starts with a story of a real-life disciplinary situation. Afterward, the story's details will be used to highlight the critical points of the chapter.

A PRACTICAL EXAMPLE OF A DISCIPLINARY INCIDENT

Full disclosure: The disciplinary incident described here is real, but enough details have been changed to ensure that it's not clear who it references. Student privacy is a critically important part of the disciplinary process, and it's important to respect that privacy here.

The incident takes place in a middle school. While it's certainly not the most serious disciplinary incident a principal might deal with, it involves a weapon and is therefore a reasonably big deal.

The incident starts when an assistant principal is told by a student that an eighth grader, who will be referred to as John, has been bragging that he has brought a knife to school. The first step is to understand the details of the claim, so the assistant principal, joined by the principal, interviews the student who overheard the comment. They learn that the student did not actually see a knife; she just overheard John speaking about it during lunch.

The two administrators then ask the witness a number of questions, including the names of other students who had been sitting at the table during lunch, and verification as to whether or not any threats were made referencing the knife.

Before the witness leaves, she is told three things. First of all, she is thanked for coming forward; her sense of responsibility for school safety means a lot. Second, the administrators let her know that they will be calling her parents later to inform them about the conversation with her, but that she is not in any type of trouble. And finally, she is told not to mention the interview to anyone else, and not to mention to anyone else what she overheard. The administrators assure her that it is fine to tell her parents all about the situation when she gets home, but she needs to stay quiet for the rest of the school day.

At this point, the principal and assistant principal look up which class John is currently in and go to get him. The school secretary calls the classroom and asks the teacher to send him to the main office, but the administrators are waiting for him as he walks out of the classroom door. He is then escorted to the assistant principal's office. While the principal waits with John, the assistant principal goes to his locker to clean it out and bring everything back to the office. The assistant principal also calls the classroom and checks with the teacher to make sure John has not left anything in the classroom.

The principal then informs John that there is reason to believe that he is in possession of something that he shouldn't have and that he is about to be searched, along with his bookbag and all the rest of his possessions. Naturally, John wants to know what they're looking for.

"I didn't do anything, I don't have anything. What are you looking for? You can't just go into my bag without my permission! What is this about?"

The principal makes it very clear to John that he does, in fact, have the right to search his bag without his permission, and then does so. After thoroughly checking his bookbag and all of his books, the principal doesn't find anything.

The next step is to search John. He hems and haws a bit but is generally cooperative. After turning out his pockets, he is then told to take off his shoes and pull down his socks. At this point, John becomes clearly agitated. Rather than handing over his shoes, he hesitates.

"Here, I can show you that there's nothing in there."

That comment gets the principal's Spidey sense tingling. He makes it clear to John that he needs to hand over his shoes, which he reluctantly does. Inside one of them is a switchblade knife with about a three-inch blade. After setting the knife aside (well out of John's reach), the principal finishes the search, finding nothing else.

While the assistant principal and the principal have been searching John, the other assistant principal has also been busy. He has been interviewing other students who were sitting at the cafeteria table and who might have overheard

John mention the knife. The primary concern with these interviews is to determine whether or not John made any threats. In those interviews, the other assistant principal is very circumspect. He doesn't ask, "Did John threaten you with a knife today at lunch?" Instead, he asks questions such as "Today at lunch, who were you sitting with? Do you remember anybody saying anything that caught your attention? Did anybody say anything that worried you?"

After finding the knife, the principal interviews John. The principal wants to know why he brought the knife to school, and what he did with it once he got there. Based on all of the interviews, the principal doesn't find any evidence that John threatened anyone, or that he had any plans to use the knife. There's nothing to suggest that he was afraid of any other students and wanted the knife for self-defense; instead, it seems as though he simply wants to impress people with what a tough kid he is.

After the search, there's still a lot to do. First of all, the principal calls John's parents and explains what happened. The principal lets them know that they need to come to school right away to get John, and that he will be suspended out of school pending a disciplinary hearing. The parents are cooperative and apologetic.

The next call is to the police. Possession of a weapon on a school campus can be a state crime in addition to being against school rules, and school administrators are obligated to report crimes occurring on school grounds to the police. This school is fortunate to have a School Resource Office (SRO)—a police officer who's assigned part-time to work at the school—so the administrators have someone they know well who also understands the school.

When John's parents arrive, the principal meets with them and explains the details of what occurred. The principal makes sure to ask them if they have any questions, and gives them his contact information so that they can follow up if they have any questions after speaking with their son. The principal then introduces the parents to the SRO, who explains to them what the next steps will be with the police and possible criminal charges.

After John and his parents leave, the principal and assistant principals call the parents of the students who were interviewed. The principal makes sure to call the parents of the first child who came forward, who want to know the name of the student who claimed to have a knife. The principal explains that he can't share that information with her, but that they are more than welcome to ask their daughter the same question. They also have concerns about John potentially retaliating against their daughter; the principal makes it clear that at no point was the daughter's name mentioned to any other student, and they worked to keep the situation very discreet. The principal assures them, however, that if they have any additional concerns after speaking with their daughter, they should contact him.

The next day the principal holds a formal disciplinary hearing with John and his parents. The hearing is held at school, but after the school day has ended. During the hearing, the principal reviews the details of what occurred, gives John an opportunity to speak, and asks his parents for their thoughts and feedback. After the meeting, the principal meets with the assistant principals, they review the local School Board policy on possession of weapons on campus, and they finalize a disciplinary decision, which involves a suspension from school of multiple days. The principal writes an e-mail to the parents attaching a formal letter with all of the information and mails them paper copies.

In addition, John's guidance counselor is asked to contact his teachers and put together a packet of work for him to complete at home while he's suspended. The principal makes sure that the parents know that the school will be holding a reintegration meeting with John when he returns to school, which they are welcome to attend. The principal also makes clear to them that, when John returns, there will be a behavior contract in place, and that this contract may include daily searches upon his arrival at school.

HOW THE SCHOOL DISCIPLINE PROCESS WORKS

There are three big pieces to any disciplinary situation: the investigation, interactions with parents, and the disciplinary decision. The next chapter, chapter 7, is entirely devoted to disciplinary decisions (the part that tends to worry parents the most!). But it's important that you are also familiar with the process leading up to those decisions. Especially if your child gets into trouble, you need a framework for understanding what the school should be doing.

The Disciplinary Investigation

Experienced school administrators will likely be involved (unfortunately) in hundreds of student disciplinary incidents during their careers, and it can feel like you've been transported into a *Law and Order* or *CSI* episode. The same general rules apply: you are trying to retroactively figure out what happened, there is a prescribed process, the people involved have certain rights (although students' rights are more restricted than those of adults in general society), evidence is key, and there are plenty of places where things can go wrong.

Here are the most important concepts that parents should understand about disciplinary investigations:

- Due process
- Collecting evidence

- Interviewing witnesses
- Search and seizure
- The role of police

Due Process

All students should be afforded due process during a disciplinary investigation. That means that administrators should be following procedural rules, that disciplinary decisions should not be made arbitrarily, and that students have the ability to know what they are being accused of. An administrator cannot simply say, "I think you did something you shouldn't, so I am giving you detention this afternoon."

This does not mean, however, that administrators need to share all of their information with a student. In the example of John, the principal told John that he was concerned that John was in possession of something that he shouldn't have, and that he needed to be searched as a result. The principal was under no obligation to tell John that he thought John had a knife. He was also under no obligation to tell John where he received his information. There certainly needed to be justifications for those actions, but the principal didn't need to share them with John right away.

Collecting Evidence

The key piece to an investigation—and to any disciplinary decision—is evidence. Unless there is a videotape that clearly shows everything that happened in a situation (which is pretty rare, but not impossible), administrators will try to piece together a picture of an event based on incomplete information collected after the fact. This means talking to students, talking to staff, reviewing video footage (if it exists), reviewing social media messages, and so on.

Collecting evidence can take a while and require a lot of work. Students frequently lie about what happened (to protect themselves or their friends), and even honest students are notoriously bad at accurately remembering or reporting what occurred (it is not uncommon for three different witnesses to give three varying accounts of an event). Smartphones are both the bane and boon of disciplinary situations. They can lead to a lot of trouble (especially when students send inappropriate messages or pictures to each other), but they can also help solve some situations. For example, if two students plan to fight each other in a private spot of the building (which does, unfortunately, happen sometimes), only to have another student videotape the fight with their phone, having a copy of that video makes it a pretty open and shut case.

Interviewing Witnesses

Probably the biggest piece of an investigation is interviewing student witnesses. This can be complicated by a lot of factors. As mentioned previously, students can have a difficult time accurately remembering something that they saw or heard (this is especially true of younger students), and many students will change their stories to protect themselves or their friends. Additionally, students can have a difficult time distinguishing between what they personally witnessed (they saw it or heard it themselves) and what they heard from others (i.e., passing along a rumor as fact).

Finally, the simple act of interviewing students can draw attention to a private situation and muddy the waters. In the story of John, the initial witness was specifically asked not to mention the interview to anyone other than her parents. Additionally, when one of the assistant principals interviewed other students, he was very circumspect in his questions. The fact is, when one student speaks to an administrator, other students want to know what's going on, and the spread of resulting rumors and gossip can complicate the investigatory process. It's not unusual to have random students attempt to insert themselves into an investigation, claiming to have important information when they really just want to be part of the drama.

Search and Seizure

In John's story, the principal searched his bookbag, everything from his locker, and him. This is an entirely legal practice and has been upheld over and over again by the courts. But that doesn't mean that school administrators can search any kid any time they want.

Out in the adult world, where police officers conduct searches, the legal threshold is "probable cause." But school administrators have a much lower legal threshold. In order to conduct a search of a student, a school administrator (and it should always be school administrators—teachers should not be searching kids) needs what is called "reasonable suspicion."

There is plenty of information available online to outline different scenarios either upheld or shot down by the courts (just search the phrase "reasonable suspicion in schools"), but administrators regularly need to make judgment calls on whether to search or not. In the case of John, a witness directly overhearing another student mention possession of a knife clearly meets the threshold of "reasonable suspicion." In contrast, a student simply reporting a rumor that had been circulating, but without having experienced anything first-hand, would most likely not.

The intrusiveness of a search can also vary. In John's case, the principal was looking for a dangerous weapon and the seriousness of that offense justified a relatively intrusive search. Imagine an alternative (but still real-life) scenario in which a female student has been accused of stealing $20, but a nonintrusive search fails to turn anything up. Someone suggests to the principal that a female staff member check the student's bra to see if the money is hidden there. A search of that type would be a horrible idea: the level of intrusiveness would only be justified in an extremely serious circumstance, and certainly not by the loss of $20.

As a general rule, however, school administrators have broad discretion to search students and their possessions when they have reasonable suspicion. Backpacks, books, shoes, even cars are fair game when the threshold is met. Cell phones are a bit trickier. If an administrator has reasonable suspicion that a student recorded something inappropriate on her phone, or communicated an inappropriate message on her phone, then a search of the phone might be justified. But administrators do not have the right to go on general fishing expeditions, scrolling through a student's private messages and content.

Administrators can also conduct random searches that do not target specific students. For example, administrators can search students' bookbags and purses prior to admittance to a school dance, or administrators can conduct searches of random lockers (so long as they actually do search a number of lockers, and don't "randomly" decide to just search one in particular).

Role of Police

Because students can break laws as well as school rules, it's possible that police can become involved in a student disciplinary investigation. The ways in which police interact with students on campus will depend on the state laws, district policies, and school practices defining those interactions. In those situations, however, there are a couple effective practices that should be observed:

- Police shouldn't interview a student below the age of eighteen without explicit parent permission (specific state laws and district or school rules may apply).
- When an alleged crime has occurred off campus and has no connection to the campus (e.g., a house break-in on the weekend), police should not interview students about it at school. It can sometimes be tempting for police to access kids at school because they know where they will be, but the best practice is for off-campus incidents to be dealt with off campus to avoid blurring the role of the school.
- Whenever possible, schools should build relationships with their local police departments, and provide opportunities for police officers to be on campus and interact with students in a non-investigatory capacity.

This helps police officers build relationships with students and staff and strengthens the partnership between schools and law enforcement officials.

In the story of John, the police were involved because his possession of a knife on campus constituted a possible crime. John was never interviewed by a police officer without his parents being present, and the principal took the time to explain to his parents how their interactions with the police were likely to play out.

In general, schools want to be able to collaborate effectively with local police—the school-police relationship represents a critically important partnership in helping to keep kids and adults safe in schools. But it is important for there to be clear rules and expectations for how that relationship should function. If a police officer ever does interact with your child at school in an investigatory capacity (whether it's because your child is a victim, a witness, or a suspect to a crime), you should be kept in the loop on that interaction, and be apprised of the school and district rules that govern that interaction.

Interactions with Parents during the Disciplinary Process

So far this chapter has looked at how disciplinary investigations work. But how should administrators be interacting with you, the parent, while the investigation plays out? Should administrators talk to parents before interviewing their child? What is an administrator's responsibility for keeping parents in the loop, and what sorts of information should administrators be sharing with parents?

If you ever get a call from an administrator about a disciplinary incident—whether because your child is a victim, a witness, or a suspect—you are likely to have lots of questions. In some cases, there are rules to what administrators can and can't tell you. In other cases, there are parent communication practices that are not so much rules, but rather guidelines for what *should* occur. If your child is involved in a disciplinary situation, the following information will help you better understand how the school should be interacting with you.

Interviewing Students without a Parent's Permission

In the situation with John, the administrators ended up interviewing a bunch of students, and they did not contact any parents until the interviews were concluded and the investigation had largely been resolved. This is common and necessary, but it can sometimes frustrate parents. Especially for younger children, or for students caught up in a serious disciplinary situation, parents might take offense that an administrator talked to their child without informing them ahead of time or securing their permission.

Schools are considered to function in loco parentis, in place of the parent, while children are at school. Because administrators are tasked with maintaining school safety, they have pretty broad discretion when it comes to investigating a disciplinary situation, and they are typically under no obligation to inform parents, or to receive their permission, before speaking to a child. In fact, informing parents ahead of time could impede an investigation, especially if a parent wants to protect her child by disallowing administrators to speak to them.

That does not mean, however, that administrators can simply do whatever they want. Administrators should be professional when speaking with students, and should never threaten or coerce students during an investigation. Interviews with students can sometimes get heated, especially with older students who are accused of something serious, but administrators still need to remain professional in their language and approach.

Depending on the situation, it can be advisable to have more than one adult present when an interview takes place. This is especially true if a child is young, has limited English, or has a disability that could inhibit his ability to understand and respond to questions effectively. In those cases, it might make sense (although is probably not required) to have an additional administrator, a guidance counselor, an ESL (English as a Second Language) teacher, or a special education teacher present while the student is questioned.

The one big exception, as mentioned earlier, is interviews with police officers. Unless state laws and district policies explicitly allow it, police officers should not interview students on school grounds without explicit permission from a parent. In cases of extreme emergency (e.g., concerns that there is a firearm or explosive device on campus), police may need to bypass this safeguard. Outside of those exceptional situations, however, you should never hear that a police officer spoke with your child about a criminal investigation without your express knowledge and approval beforehand.

Communicating with Parents during a Disciplinary Process

While school administrators frequently need to interview students without a parent's permission, that does not mean that parents are completely out of the loop. When investigating the situation with John, the administrators made a point of calling all of the parents of students who had been interviewed. It is generally not a rule that administrators have to call the parents of interviewed students, but it represents a good practice.

When a student is a victim, there should be quick, proactive communication with parents. Particularly if a student has been injured, parents need to be informed right away. Had John actually used his knife to injure another student, the principal would not have waited for the investigation to conclude before contacting the parents of an injured student.

The parents of a victim should also be kept in the loop on how an investigation is progressing. This does not mean that the parents of a victim have a right to know all the details of an investigation—in fact, administrators are required by law to keep many details private (more on that in the following pages). But especially when a disciplinary situation involves physical injury or concerns for ongoing safety, it's important for administrators to be in communication with the parents of a victim.

The parents of a disciplined student should also expect lots of communication, some of it potentially required by law (e.g., Title IX laws set certain communication requirements). Administrators should provide the parents of disciplined students with a clear summary of what occurred and why their child is being disciplined, along with references to the appropriate school rules or district policies. For more serious offenses that involve a suspension out of school, it is likely that state law or district policy will require formal, written communication about the disciplinary situation, including information about an appeal process (if one exists for the given level of discipline). In John's situation with the knife, the principal made sure to provide formal documentation to the parents, both via e-mail (to get the information there quickly) and via hard copy through the mail.

In exceptional situations, it may also be appropriate for school administrators to communicate with the parents of students who were not directly impacted. For example, if offensive graffiti is discovered painted in the gym, a principal might want to inform the larger community. Or if a large number of students are caught drinking on campus, and everyone seems to be talking about it, a principal may want to proactively inform the whole parent community about how it's being addressed. As a general rule, however, the parents of students who are not involved in a disciplinary situation should have no expectation that the school will tell them about it. But when rumors are flying or a principal wants to reinforce a message of school safety, she may decide that it's worth it to send a message out to everyone.

Information That Schools Can and Can't Share

Some common questions from parents, especially the parents of student victims, are, "Well, what punishment did you give the perpetrator?" "What exactly happened?" and "Who was involved?"

There is a federal law called FERPA—the Family Education Rights and Privacy Act—that states that student educational records are private and cannot be shared without the express, written permission of a student's parents.[1] Disciplinary records are considered to be part of a student's educational records. This means that, when a parent wants to know about disciplinary consequences given to anyone other than their own child, school administrators should not be sharing that information.

In addition, administrators should not be sharing the names of students involved in a disciplinary incident: the victim(s), witness(es), or perpetrator(s). The parents of a disciplined child will sometimes want to know who the students were who served as witnesses or want to see copies of what they said. In a court of law, that information might be available, but it is not in a school disciplinary investigation (in recent years, Title IX investigations are an exception). Even when a disciplined student is on social media telling the whole world, "Hey, I just got suspended for doing this!" administrators should still avoid using the student's name when talking about the incident.

So, an administrator should never share information that might violate student privacy laws. At the same time, parents often have a reasonable right to understand how a disciplinary situation is being handled, especially if their child was a victim, and there is information that administrators *can* share.

For example, an administrator shouldn't say, "I just suspended that student from school for two days." What an administrator could say, however, is, "According to our student handbook, that type of offense typically results in an out-of-school suspension of one to three days." It can mean walking a fine line between protecting student privacy and reassuring parents that student safety is being maintained. But when you are concerned about a situation and have questions, go ahead and reach out to an administrator: if they can tell you something, they will, and if they can't tell you, they won't.

NOTE

1. For more information about FERPA, your best resource is probably the federal government's website at https://www2.ed.gov/policy/gen/guid/fpco/ferpa/index.html.

Chapter 7

What Are Common Disciplinary Consequences and What Do They Mean for Students?

The previous chapter looked at disciplinary investigations and the types of communication that parents should expect during an investigation. But for many students and parents, the most stress-inducing, frustrating, and eye-opening part of student discipline are the actual consequences.

This is especially true when the consequences are, well, consequential. Most people can live with a time-out or an after-school detention, maybe even a day sitting in the in-school suspension (ISS) room (although some kids and parents will still fight those tooth and nail). But when a student faces the prospect of being suspended from school, panic can set in.

This chapter looks at the details of disciplinary consequences. It starts by walking you through the typical range of consequences that a student might encounter, providing some examples of the types of behaviors that might lead to them. Next, the chapter looks at the long-term impact of discipline: how schools track student behavior, the responsibilities of schools to report disciplinary information to outside institutions, and the disciplinary impact on, as the Violent Femmes liked to say, your "permanent record."

THE RANGE OF DISCIPLINARY CONSEQUENCES

While this chapter is focused on negative student behavior, and the disciplinary outcomes that can result, not all behavioral consequences have to be punitive. Plenty of teachers and schools attempt to reward positive student behavior, using everything from a classroom prize box to, in some strange-but-true scenarios, actual cash.[1] While that is certainly a worthy topic for discussion, and likely a more uplifting one, the focus here is on negative behaviors and the disciplinary consequences that can result.

Schools have a range of consequences that they can use to influence and address student behavior, and those consequences tend to fall into six general categories:

- Verbal reprimands
- Academic penalties
- Loss of membership or privileges
- Time-out during the school day
- Time owed outside the school day
- Removal from school

Verbal Reprimands

Verbal warnings and reprimands are pretty common in schools. They can range from the relatively benign "Ben, I need you to knock that off and pay attention" to the more serious "The next time something like this happens, I am putting you out of school."

Teachers are likely to have a formalized set of expectations and rules in their classrooms, and the first violation of those rules is often met with a verbal reprimand, as opposed to an actual consequence. Particularly in the younger grades, teachers may have a system to track verbal reprimands; for example, students given a warning might need to change their "color" from green to yellow, or yellow to red, on a chart in the room or on their desk.

Verbal reprimands are pretty common; after all, put enough kids together for an extended period of time and some of them are just naturally going to get a little squirrely. They are often not reported to parents, especially in middle or high school. A pattern of minor behavior might lead to a formal consequence, but many teachers might start with a call home rather than a time-out or detention.

Academic Penalties

While this topic might be controversial to some, it shouldn't be: simply put, students should never be given an academic penalty for a nonacademic behavior. Here's a description of what that means.

If a student cheats on a paper or test, that is an academic behavior. It therefore deserves an academic penalty, usually a reduced grade or no credit on the assignment. Depending on the classroom or school rules, it might also lead to an additional consequence, such as an after-school detention.

But students should not be given an academic penalty, such as a reduced grade, for a nonacademic behavior. For example, if a student uses inappropriate language in class, that should not result in the student losing

10 points on the next quiz. He could be assigned a detention, sent to the main office, get a phone call home—all of those are fine because they are nonacademic penalties for a nonacademic action.

One tricky, gray area is homework. There are two elements to completing homework. First is the academic component; in other words, the extent to which a homework assignment is completed accurately. The second piece is the behavioral component; in other words, whether the homework is actually completed. Some would argue that homework completion should not count against a student's grade because the act of completing or not completing homework represents a nonacademic behavior. But in most schools, it is considered perfectly appropriate for teachers to assign grades for homework, and to therefore penalize a student academically when they do not complete it (although homework probably shouldn't comprise a substantial portion of a student's grade, probably no more than 5–10 percent).

Aside from the possible exception of homework, however, students should not receive academic penalties for nonacademic behaviors.

Loss of Membership or Privileges

Especially as students get older, they often have the opportunity to participate in extracurricular activities, such as sports, clubs, or school events. It's possible that inappropriate behavior could impact students' ability to do so.

The first example is formalized school groups or clubs. This could include sports teams, the National Honor Society, the chess club, or the school play. In some cases, these groups may have specific rules or expectations around student behavior. For example, membership in the National Honor Society is based on a set of core principles, and violation of those principles can lead to removal from the group. Similarly, a school may have a rule that students are not allowed to participate in any after-school clubs if they have received a certain level of disciplinary consequence during the school year (e.g., students who have been suspended from school at any point during the year might be disallowed from participation in certain extracurricular opportunities).

The key thing with these sorts of consequences is that they need to be explicitly described in a student handbook or in organization by-laws, and the consequences must be applied uniformly. The director of the school play can't kick out one kid for having received ISS but keep another student who received the same disciplinary consequence (even if that student plays the lead role and it's the day before the play opens). If your child ever receives these sorts of consequences, read the student handbook or by-laws carefully to make sure that the consequences are supported by the rules.

The area where this can be especially controversial is in connection with sports. Either at the district or the state level, it's common to see rules specifying that student-athletes are not allowed to possess or consume alcohol or illegal drugs at any time during the school year, in or out of school. In practice, this means that, if a kid is busted by the police for having beer in his car on the weekend, and that kid happens to be an athlete, he could lose the opportunity to participate in athletics for a period of time.

Naturally, kids don't like to be prevented from playing sports that they're passionate about, and parents don't like to see their kids sanctioned this way. If something like this happens to your child, read the rules very carefully.

The other example in this general category is participation in after-school events. For instance, a middle school might have a rule that students are not allowed to attend the Eighth Grade Formal if they have been suspended from school at any point during the school year. Once again, these rules would need to be clearly spelled out in school documents, and the rules would need to be applied uniformly.

Time-Out during the School Day

This is one of the most common consequences, especially for younger students. A "time out" can range from sitting out an activity for a few minutes, to being sent to the front office during a class period, to spending an entire day in an ISS room. At the nonserious end, students can be given a short time-out for a range of minor behaviors: heated words on the playground, being too chatty in class, or throwing a piece of food at the cafeteria table. At the more serious end, students can be put into ISS (essentially, sitting in a monitored room for the whole day) for making threatening comments, minor physical aggression, harassing or bullying behavior, and so on.

Elementary school teachers may or may not inform parents about a time-out, depending on the circumstances. If a student gets worked up on the playground and has to sit out for a couple minutes, there may not be a note home. If it happens repeatedly, though, parents should probably be informed. And if the student makes it to an administrator's office for a time-out, parents should find out about it.

For middle and high school students who are kept out of class for an extended period of time (a class period, half-day, or full-day in ISS), parents need to be informed.

It was mentioned earlier that students should not be given academic consequences for nonacademic behavior, and that applies here as well. When a student is removed from instructional time, the student needs to have the opportunity to make up any missed work. In other words, if a student is assigned a day of ISS on the day of a big math test, the student can't be given a zero as a test grade: he needs the opportunity to make up the test.

Schools also have to be careful that they are following district policies and state laws around seclusion. Having a child sit out of an activity for a period of time, or even miss a full-day of classes, is not a problem in-and-of-itself, but the way in which it is handled makes a big difference. For example, a student sitting in a monitored ISS room is not being secluded, but a student put into a closet by herself definitely is.

Finally, schools have to be careful about when they give students time-out. If an elementary student gets worked up while on the playground, sitting out of recess for a while makes sense. But if a student got into trouble earlier in the day during a writing activity, the teacher should not be taking recess away as a consequence. Similarly, if a middle school student acts up during math class, taking her out of her art class is not appropriate.

Time Owed Outside the School Day

This is another common consequence, especially at the middle and high school levels. Minor disciplinary offenses can often earn a student "detention" after school (or before school, if a school has a later start time). Some schools even put in place "Saturday school," when students who have committed more serious offenses serve their punishment on a Saturday (this is often used in lieu of ISS to limit the amount of class time that students miss).

After-school detentions are a common consequence imposed by secondary teachers, and they are also a go-to penalty handed out by secondary school administrators. After-school detentions can be given for a wide range of relatively minor behaviors: inappropriate language in class, repeated classroom disruptions, being in the wrong place in the building, and so on.

There are two big challenges to these types of consequences. The first is transportation: if a student has to stay after school, then the parents may need to arrange alternative transportation for their child to get home, especially if their child is used to riding a school bus. Teachers and administrators generally view this as a parent's problem to solve. There might be a little wiggle room to help accommodate a parent's busy schedule, but schools are generally not willing to be too flexible.

The other big challenge is follow-through. A school has pretty close to total control over where a student will be during the school day, so a time-out during the day is supremely enforceable. But it is hard for a school to *make* a student stay after school. It's not uncommon for a high school student to basically say to an administrator, "Screw you, I'm not staying after school to serve your detention." A school's only response is to up the ante: if you won't serve your thirty minutes of detention, then the school will now impose an even bigger penalty. In some cases, a stubborn student can resist detentions to the point that they end up being assigned a full day of ISS for what was, in the beginning, a pretty minor offense.

This is where communication and collaboration with parents is key. Schools will almost always inform parents of an after-school detention, and schools rely on parents to work with them to get a student to serve a consequence. After-school punishments are infinitely better than punishments during school because they minimize the amount of missed class time. So, if your child is assigned an after-school detention—or, more significantly, Saturday school—please try to work with the school to ensure that your child serves the consequence.

Removal from School

A school's most significant disciplinary action is removal from school, commonly referred to as an out-of-school suspension (or OSS). The extreme form of OSS is expulsion, in which a student is permanently removed from a school.

There are certainly students who would prefer to be suspended out of school to an ISS, because OSS feels like a day off. And parents will sometimes ask why the two levels of discipline aren't reversed: Why isn't ISS considered the max penalty given how much students tended to loathe it (it is, after all, incredibly boring to sit in the same room all day, with no one to talk to and nothing to do but class assignments)?

State constitutions grant students the right to a public education. When a school suspends a student out of school, they are essentially taking away that right for a period of time. As much as some students might not mind the prospect of being removed from school for a day or two, it is a much more consequential action from a "rights" perspective.

For this reason, schools must tread carefully when putting a student out of school. There must be compelling evidence to justify the decision, and schools need to follow the due process carefully. There are also more specific administrative requirements for OSSs, including formalized processes for notifying parents of an OSS decision and potential appeal options.

This is especially true for OSSs in excess of ten days, often referred to as long-term suspensions. For students who have an Individualized Education Plan, or IEP (i.e., are part of the special education program), there are additional administrative requirements for longer suspensions. But for any student who is put out of school for an extended period of time, here are a couple important points to consider:

- Schools and districts remain responsible for a student's education, even while they are suspended. Schools can meet this obligation in a variety of

ways—sending work packets home, relying on online classes, employing tutors to work with a student at the public library—and the details will depend on state and district rules. But when students are suspended, the school and district typically still have an obligation to move their education forward.
- A formal appeals process typically only exists for suspensions greater than ten days. These appeals will most likely go to the Superintendent or the School Board/Committee, depending on district policies. For parents whose child is suspended for an extended period of time, reading the rules very carefully is critical (and those rules should be found in the Student Handbook).

Removal from school should only occur when a student has behaved in very inappropriate ways, causing a significant disturbance to the learning environment or endangering student and school safety. Physical fights are suspendable offenses, as are drug- or alcohol-related behaviors (e.g., being in possession at school, under the influence at school, or selling or buying at school). Sexual harassment or assault could lead to significant time-out of school, as could serious threats. Possession of a weapon is definitely a suspendable offense, as was true in the story of John in the previous chapter. Threats or aggressive behaviors toward staff members are also a quick way to be put out of school. In some instances, a continuing pattern of lesser behavior could lead to an OSS, but it would still need to be pretty serious behavior (e.g., an ongoing pattern of using inappropriate language in class, multiple instances of harassing behavior, or a pattern of threatening language).

THIS WILL (MOST LIKELY NOT) GO DOWN ON YOUR PERMANENT RECORD

Here's a scenario that will feel familiar to any high school principal: the principal is meeting with a parent whose child has done something relatively serious and is receiving a serious consequence (e.g., being suspended from school for a day or two). The facts are not in question—the kid has clearly done what he was accused of doing—but the parent is trying to reduce the impact of the discipline.

Inevitably, at some point during the conversation the parent gets around to the real reason for the meeting: they're worried that the record of the disciplinary consequence will impact their child's ability to get into college. But once the principal explains to them that the school does not share disciplinary information with colleges, except in the most extreme circumstances, the concern disappears. "Oh, this won't impact him getting into college? Then definitely, he fully deserves to be suspended for doing such a boneheaded thing."

Schools and school districts do tend to track disciplinary information, and that information can follow them from one school to the next. But disciplinary information is almost never shared with outside agencies (police can be the big exception if a crime has been committed). That doesn't mean that serious disciplinary behavior can't filter out at times, but that only tends to happen in rare circumstances.

How Discipline Records Are Tracked

Most schools or districts will have an in-house way of tracking more serious incidents of student misbehavior. This will likely be electronic, tied into a back-end student information system. The electronic information will also likely follow a student from one school to the next within a district, especially as a student moves from elementary to middle to high school.

So, if a student gets into trouble with an administrator, the administrator can very likely look back at the student's record to see if the student has ever gotten into trouble before. This information is, however, most likely kept pretty confidential. School administrators have access to disciplinary information, but teachers generally do not. There are certainly word-of-mouth and in-house reputations as students move from one teacher to the next, but parents do not need to worry about everyone in a school having access to their child's discipline information.

And while most schools will maintain a hard copy of a student's school records, this generally does not include disciplinary information. Report cards, standardized test scores, and special education paperwork: all of this information will be kept in a student's in-house folder, but discipline is most likely not in there. And once a student leaves a school, the records follow him. Schools tend to maintain only bare-bones information about students once they leave, and that "permanent record" almost certainly excludes disciplinary information.

Sharing Discipline Records Externally

The previous chapter mentioned FERPA, the federal law that protects student privacy. That law means that schools can't share a student's educational record with outside institutions without parents' written consent. So, by law, schools can't just go sharing information with external institutions.

When it comes to colleges, universities, summer job opportunities, or scholarship organizations, schools will almost certainly not share anything related to student behavior. Colleges or universities might ask students to self-disclose discipline information, but those organizations are not interested in knowing that a student served detention once in seventh grade for making paper airplanes in the back of the room. Outside institutions *may* want to know if a student has been severely disciplined for offenses such as drug dealing, bringing a firearm onto campus, or assaulting a staff member. But even in those instances, schools are unlikely to be the ones to share the details of the information.

One sort of exception to all of this is instances in which a student transfers from one school to another. Let's say your family moves from California to Oklahoma, your child's school records from California will need to be sent to the new school. But this only happens after you have given your consent for the records to be transferred, and there's a good chance that the information sent to the new school will not include any detailed disciplinary information.

Other Ways That Discipline Can Nevertheless Filter Out

Schools do not generally share disciplinary information with outside institutions. But that doesn't mean that serious disciplinary incidents will never get out. For example, colleges and universities do expect a high school to let them know if something substantial has happened to a student's educational progress from the time they were accepted into the college up to the time they graduate from high school. So, if a student is suspended from school for the last semester of her senior year for bringing a gun onto campus, the high school has an obligation to let a college know that she is no longer taking classes physically at the school. They will likely not explain why, but a college will pick up pretty quickly on that red flag.

Students also frequently need recommendations from school staff when applying to different external organizations. While a staff member will almost definitely not say, "Johnny once got suspended for bringing a knife to school," recommendations can hint at issues with behavior.

Administrators may also have off-the-record conversations with each other in extreme circumstances. If a new student shows up at a school in March, and he comes to the school under some shady circumstances, chances are the new principal is going to pick up the phone and call the former principal. That principal is unlikely to say, "Yeah, that guy's bad news, we suspended him for selling pot on campus." But he might mention that it's a good idea to keep an eye on the student when he's not in class and to check regularly to see if his pupils seem dilated or if he seems to be carrying around an especially large wad of cash.

NOTE

1. https://edlabs.harvard.edu/news/14-schools-named-dc-program-motivate-students-cash

Chapter 8

Your Child Got Into Trouble with a Teacher—Now What?

Previous chapters looked at disciplinary rules, processes, and consequences. This chapter will now focus on what to do when your child actually gets into trouble with a teacher. The next chapter will then discuss the more serious situations when your child gets into trouble with a school administrator.

Most parents' experience with student discipline will be at the classroom level. This level of discipline isn't typically that serious—after all, if it were serious it would get bumped up to an assistant principal or principal. But it can still be stress-inducing. The advice to help you navigate these situations falls into four general categories:

- Understand the situation and the concern
- Listen to your child
- Work with the teacher
- Escalate when necessary

UNDERSTAND THE SITUATION AND THE CONCERN

When a child gets into trouble with his teacher, parents usually find out through one of two ways: the teacher contacts the parents directly (via e-mail, a note in the "home communication folder," a phone call, etc.) or the kid spills the beans when he gets home—"Mom, I got moved to yellow in class today!"

As a parent, your first step is to understand the details of what happened. If the teacher contacts you directly, read what he said very carefully. Some teachers will provide plenty of detail in an e-mail or note, making sure parents have a clear picture of what occurred. Other teachers may keep it short, writing a simple, "Johnny had to move his color to yellow today, please talk to him about it."

Before you can respond effectively to a disciplinary situation, you need the full picture. If the teacher only gave you a limited sense of what occurred, or if your child is the one who brought home the information, reach out to the teacher to get a better sense of the details.

Your communication with the teacher should be very neutral—this is not the time to justify or excuse your child's behavior, or to make any accusations toward the teacher. Instead, your goal is simply to understand what happened. A good opening to a note, e-mail, or phone call is, "I am very sorry for what occurred in class today. In order to work effectively with Johnny on this behavior, I want to make sure I understand the details of what occurred." From there, focus on a couple questions:

- What exact behavior(s) did your child exhibit? If the teacher indicated that he "kept being disruptive in class," you want to know exactly what those disruptions looked like. Was your child calling out answers repeatedly without raising his hand? Was he dancing a jig during a math lesson? Similarly, if the teacher says that he was "disrespectful," you want to know what exactly he said or did. "Disrespectful" can mean anything from a quiet giggle to openly mock the teacher's new wardrobe. You want to know as specifically as possible what your child did.
- What rules or expectations were broken? Is there a rule that students may not speak without raising their hands first and being called on? Are students expected to have their cell phones stored in their bookbags at all times?
- Was this a one-off event, or a pattern of behavior that the teacher has noticed? Is this the first time your child has gotten into trouble for this behavior, or is it just the first time you are hearing about it?
- How serious is the concern? If your child is a little too chatty in class, that's a different situation than if your child is regularly making inappropriate and suggestive sexual comments to other students.

Again, be very careful to be neutral in asking any questions. If you say to the teacher, "Well, do you have a class rule against answering questions without raising your hand?" that can come across as aggressive and accusatory. Instead, rephrase that sort of question as, "I want to make sure I can help Johnny clearly understand your expectations going forward. Can you please let me know what your rules are around asking questions in class?"

LISTEN TO YOUR CHILD

Parents have to walk a careful line when speaking with their children about disciplinary incidents that happen in school. On the one hand, you want to support your child as she deals with the emotional reaction to getting into trouble. On the other hand, you want to be careful to reinforce classroom rules and the teacher's authority. A reaction of, "That's ridiculous that the teacher yelled at you for such a silly thing!" might well endear you to your child for the moment but could also embolden your child to continue the same behavior in the future.

To that end, it's recommended that you take a number of steps when speaking to your child about a disciplinary incident at school:

Ask your child to explain what happened—Have your child tell you what happened in his own words. But remember, the younger the child, the more likely he is to remember his emotions instead of objective actions; and the older the child, the more likely he is to recount only those details that paint him in the best light (and the teacher in the worst light). Listening to your child is important—it helps you better understand what happened, at least from your child's perspective, and it places you in a position to be an emotional support. But listening doesn't necessarily mean agreeing. You can commiserate with your child's emotions and situation ("I'm so sorry that this happened and you are upset"), without validating or justifying his behavior.

Balance holding your child accountable with supporting your child emotionally—Just as the threat of school consequences can deter children's behavior, the threat of consequences at home can have a similar impact. It's perfectly reasonable to impose a consequence at home when a child gets into trouble at school, but a consequence at home should be proportional to the severity of the behavior. A time-out during recess might warrant a short-term loss of access to the video game console; a day of ISS could warrant being grounded for several weeks.

On the flip side, it's important for you to help your child work through the emotional impact of getting into trouble. A kid who feels like everyone is against him will have a hard time recovering in a positive and productive way from a disciplinary situation. Children need to know that parents can be disappointed in their behaviors, while still loving them unconditionally. For a student who gets into trouble, it's important to emphasize that it isn't their mistakes that define them, but how they respond in the wake of those mistakes. Kids screw up sometimes. By framing those screw-ups as learning opportunities and chances to improve, parents can help children make better decisions in the future while maintaining a positive sense of self.

Follow up with the teacher if you still have questions—After speaking with your child about a disciplinary incident, you may have questions (even if you already heard from the teacher). If they are low-key questions, you can probably ignore them. But if the questions are substantive, make sure to follow up with the teacher.

A low-key question is one that might reflect a discrepancy in the story, but doesn't impact the situation or how you respond to it: Did your child tell the teacher "I hate this!" or did he say "This is stupid!"? Did the incident on the playground happen before snack or after snack? Substantive questions affect your deeper understanding of the situation and impact the steps you take at home or your ability to support your child. Has your child been struggling with completing assignments, and his outburst reflected frustration? Has there been an ongoing conflict with another student, and the incident at recess was the final straw? As recommended above, make sure to keep your questions to the teacher as neutral and non-accusatory as possible.

WORK WITH THE TEACHER

If your child's disciplinary situation was an isolated, low-key incident, then there probably isn't much need for additional follow-up with the teacher. For example, if your third-grade child had a one-time argument at recess with a friend, or your high school sophomore skipped his first-ever class to do some last-minute work on an important project, you can likely move on pretty quickly from the incident. That doesn't mean you ignore it, but it probably doesn't require a multi-point action plan.

If, however, your child is getting into trouble for a continuing pattern of behavior, or your child got into trouble for something more serious, it's recommended that you take some more formal steps to work with the teacher to address the behavior. Reach out to the teacher and request a conference to discuss the situation. When you meet with the teacher, focus on the following pieces of advice.

Understand the Teacher's Concerns

First, you want to know what the teacher thinks. You might be concerned that your child keeps getting into trouble for the same behavior, but the teacher sees it as relatively age-appropriate and not a big deal. Alternatively, you might think your rambunctious middle schooler is just being silly, whereas the teacher sees the behavior as inappropriate and concerning. Listen to the teacher in a nonjudgmental way, using the following questions as ways to better understand her perspective:

- What specific behaviors are you seeing in the classroom that you think we should be concerned about?

- How concerned are you about these behaviors? Do they seem pretty typical for students this age, or do you see them as especially concerning?
- Why do you think my child is exhibiting these behaviors? Do you have any guesses or theories?
- What might happen if the behaviors continue? Should I be worried about more significant consequences for my child?

Be Honest about Your Own Concerns

It may be the case that you completely understand the teacher's concerns, and you see your child as guilty of the behaviors the teacher describes. It's also possible, however, that your perspective on the situation is different. You may believe that the teacher is over-reacting to relatively minor stuff, or you might think that the teacher's own behaviors are contributing to the situation. If that's the case, then you need to decide: Can you keep your opinions to yourself, or do you feel that you need to be honest with the teacher about your own concerns?

If you see it as important to be honest with the teacher, try to be carefully and selectively honest. For example, please don't say, "It's not a big deal, I don't understand why you're making such a fuss!" Instead, you might say, "I'll be honest, I don't see those behaviors as especially problematic, but I'm also not trying to manage 20 kids at a time."

Where you probably do need to be honest with the teacher as if you see him contributing to the situation. For example, if the teacher is making sarcastic comments to your child, and your child is getting into trouble in reaction to those comments, you need to bring that up with the teacher. Again, make sure you understand the teacher's perspective on the situation—what your child labels "sarcastic" may feel perfectly appropriate to the teacher—and be especially delicate and non-accusatory in the way you frame your concerns. Rather than "Stop using so much sarcasm with my child!" you might try saying, "From Johnny's perspective, he tells us that he feels you're being sarcastic with him, and that's what he sees as contributing to the situation."

Give the Teacher the Benefit of the Doubt

Here's a common, real-life scenario: A parent meets with an administrator, all fired-up angry about her child's teacher. Listening to the parent's descriptions, one would think that the teacher has sprouted horns and is carrying around a pitchfork. All of the parent's anger, however, is based on her child's description of the teacher, not on any actual interactions with the teacher. Once the angry parent finally sits down with the teacher, it turns out that the information the child has been bringing home is pretty seriously at odds with reality.

Try to give your child's teacher the benefit of the doubt in a disciplinary situation, and make sure to listen to and understand her perspective before forming too strong an opinion about the situation.

Focus on Solutions

Your primary goal when you meet with a teacher about a disciplinary situation is to leave the meeting with some possible solutions. You want to figure out a way that you and the teacher can work together to help your child improve her behavior going forward. To do that, you need to do the following:

Agree on what behaviors need to be addressed—If the teacher simply complains that your child is "disrespectful" or "disruptive," you're going to have a tough time helping your child change his behavior. Those descriptions are simply too vague. Instead, you and the teacher need to get to a very specific definition of the problematic behaviors so that you can clearly explain and fully focus on them with your child. For example, "Speaks out in class without having been called upon" is more specific and targetable than "disruptive."

Understand how the teacher has tried to address the behavior in the past—Before coming up with a new plan to address your child's behaviors, you need to know what the teacher has already tried. It's possible that you see some of the same behaviors at home, and you've put in place a successful system to manage them that the teacher could duplicate in class. Or, maybe the teacher has been misreading your child and is trying an approach that you know is not likely to work.

Come up with a plan to manage the behaviors at school and at home—This is the key step: you and the teacher need to be working together with an agreed-upon plan to address the behaviors. Maybe every time your child calls out inappropriately in class, she loses a day of screen time at home. Maybe your child earns the opportunity to go with you to the movies if she goes a full week with no negative behaviors at school. The point is to have a plan that includes some incentives and/or disincentives that tie behavior at school to actions at home. Once a child realizes that her teacher and parent are in regular cahoots and communication, a lot of problematic behaviors tend to magically disappear.

Agree on a way to communicate regularly going forward—After coming up with a plan, you need to have an agreed-upon way to communicate with the teacher going forward. Maybe she e-mails you with a summary at the end of the week and maybe there is a daily checklist that she fills out and comes home in your child's bookbag. Whatever the system, make sure you leave the meeting having agreed upon it, and then stick to it. The key to changing your child's behavior is consistency, so maintaining consistent communication with the teacher is super important.

Share the plan with your child—The final step is to share any plan with your child. This could be something that you do with your child at home, or it could be a joint meeting with you, your child, and the teacher. For older kids, it might even be appropriate to have them participate in the initial meeting with the teacher when the plan is developed. Before you share the plan with your child, however, you need to decide whether your child has the ability to contribute to the plan, or is simply responsible for following it. Chances are your child will want the option of changing it—"Come on, mom, that's so unfair!"—so you need to decide beforehand whether your response will be, "Okay, tell me what you think would be fair changes to it," or "Tough luck, mister, your actions got you to this point, and now this is how it's going to be."

Preserve the Relationship

For better or for worse, this teacher is most likely going to be working with your child for the remainder of the school year. Even if you believe the teacher is negatively contributing to the situation, or the teacher is blowing a relatively minor thing out of proportion, it is in your child's best interests for you to preserve a positive relationship with the teacher. To that end, try to be as productive, polite, and understanding in your interactions with the teacher, even if it means biting your tongue at times.

The exception to this advice is when you believe the teacher is truly treating your child inappropriately and is causing harm to your child's emotional and/or academic well-being. In that case, it is perfectly appropriate for you to escalate the situation, even if it compromises your relationship with the teacher. Read on for advice on how to escalate when necessary.

ESCALATE WHEN NECESSARY

You have taken steps to understand your child's classroom-based disciplinary situation, and you have tried to work with the teacher to address it. But you are now truly convinced that either the disciplinary situation is a result of the teacher acting inappropriately, the teacher is disciplining your child in a way that is inappropriate, and/or the teacher's actions are harmful to your child. In that case, you should escalate the situation.

Escalating a classroom discipline situation typically means talking with an administrator. An intermediate step, especially if your child is in middle or high school, could be talking with your child's guidance counselor; either way, the process on your end should be the same. The big difference between an administrator and a guidance counselor is that administrators supervise teachers, whereas guidance counselors don't. If you're just looking for advice, then a guidance counselor might be the better route to take. If you have deeper concerns, however, or you are looking for some sort of action, then you should reach out to an administrator (typically starting with an assistant principal, if your school has one).

Here is the process to escalate:

Set up a meeting—It's recommended that you try to set up a face-to-face appointment, but a phone call could also work (for more serious concerns, meet face-to-face). In setting up the appointment, let the guidance counselor or administrator know the purpose of the meeting, make it clear that you have already spoken with the teacher about the situation, and ask the person to keep the meeting private for now. Also, make it clear that you don't want the teacher to participate in this conversation.

Explain the situation—At the meeting or during the phone conversation, provide as much detail as you can about the situation. Try to do this in as factual and nonjudgmental a way as possible. After explaining your understanding of the situation, be sure to share your concerns honestly and directly. Try to avoid especially sensitive words such as "bullying" or "harassment" (e.g., rather than saying "I think the teacher is bullying my child," you could say something like, "The teacher seems to be repeatedly using an aggressive tone with my child and treating him differently from other students in the class in a way that feels personal to him").

Make your intentions clear—This is a decision that you need to figure out before the meeting, and then explain during the meeting. What outcome are you looking for? Are you just looking to vent to someone at the school? Are you hoping for advice about what to do next? Do you expect some sort of action to be taken after the meeting?

It's not uncommon for a parent to call an administrator with concerns about a classroom discipline incident, and the conversations ended with the parent essentially saying, "Thanks for listening. I'm not asking you to do anything, I just wanted to make sure someone in a position of authority was aware of these concerns." It's also not uncommon for a parent to call an administrator just looking for some guidance and encouragement about how to meet with a teacher. But sometimes a parent calls and says, "Look, this situation is not okay with me. I need you to do something." Those are all perfectly good reasons for you to contact someone at your school—just know where your head is before you have the conversation.

Follow through on next steps—If your conversation with the guidance counselor or administrator was just a venting session, then there may be no "next steps," other than keeping an eye on your child and how things progress. But if there were some concrete things that came out of the conversation, then make sure you follow through. That might mean having an uncomfortable follow-up conversation with the teacher, but it's important for you to ensure that you don't compromise on the way your child is treated.

Chapter 9

Your Child Got Into Trouble with an Administrator—Now What?

The previous chapter talked about responding to a disciplinary situation that happens at the classroom level. This chapter looks at discipline that involves a school administrator, which typically indicates a higher level of concern.

These situations can be both confusing and frustrating. For a parent, it can feel as though school administrators are the judge, the jury, and the executioner, while parents are just helpless bystanders.

Up to a certain point, this is actually pretty accurate.

It's easy to understand a parent's frustration: another adult is taking action against *your* child, that action could have some real negative implications, and there's very little you can do about it. But the fact is, for better or for worse, parents only play a limited role when it comes to school-level discipline.

There are good reasons for that. A parent's first instinct is to defend her child—some parents are willing to bend, or even blatantly disregard the rules if it means supporting their kid. Especially when big-time consequences are on the table, parents may be less interested in seeing justice served and more interested in seeing their child protected.

But it can still be frustrating to have to sit by while everything plays out.

That does not mean, however, that parents have *no* role when school-level discipline occurs. But to involve yourself productively, you need to understand the facts and the process. You also need to understand what you can do to support your child, while still working effectively with the school.

UNDERSTAND THE FACTS AND THE PROCESS

Here's another real-life situation: An elementary school boy gets into trouble on the playground. It seems that another boy has been saying mean things to him, and one day he has had enough: he finally responds by pushing the other boy to the ground. Another student saw the boy being pushed and reports it to a teacher.

Because of his son's physical aggression, the father is called and told by the school's assistant principal that his son will spend a day in the principal's office (the elementary school equivalent of ISS).

"I completely understand," the father responds, "and please know that we do not tolerate that sort of behavior at home. Rest assured that my son will be given consequences at home." The father pauses, and then continues, "I assume, of course, that the other child will be receiving consequences as well for what he said to my son."

At this point, the conversation takes an awkward turn. It turns out that the other child is not going to be receiving any consequences. The assistant principal notes that no one else reported overhearing the mean comment, and there is no way to prove that it occurred.

"So, the other student denied that he said it? Because this isn't the first time that my son has told me about hearing mean comments from this other kid."

The assistant principal indicates that he can't get into the specifics of the investigation, and because of privacy concerns he can't share whether or not the other student has admitted to making the comment. The father begins to suspect that the assistant principal has never even questioned the other kid or spoken to any potential witnesses.

"Hold on a second. My kid is getting a day in the principal's office, a pretty big deal. But absolutely nothing is happening to the other kid, and you can't even tell me whether or not he admitted to saying something inappropriate to my son!"

The father isn't frustrated that his child is being punished—he readily understands that his son broke the school's rules and deserves a consequence. What sticks in his craw is that the school doesn't seem to have handled the process in an equitable manner.

To ensure that your child has been treated equitably in a disciplinary situation, you need to do two things: understand the disciplinary rules and ask some probing questions. The rules should be contained in the school's student handbook, and in following pages you will find a set of questions that you can ask of an administrator.

Read the Student Handbook

The student handbook is the collection of the rules governing student behavior. If your child is involved in a disciplinary incident, you will definitely want to get a copy of the student handbook and familiarize yourself with it (your child may have been given a hard copy at the beginning of the year, and there should be electronic copies available on the school and/or district website). As you read through the handbook, ask yourself some questions:

- Did the administrator follow the disciplinary process described in the handbook, and the important steps outlined in chapter 6? For example, if an administrator assigned your child a consequence without ever giving your child an opportunity to give his side of things, then due process was not followed.
- Is the way the school is handling the situation reasonable in light of the student handbook language? For example, if your child is given a day of ISS for an offense that the handbook states should be met with a single after-school detention, then the consequence doesn't match the offense.
- Is there an opportunity for appeal? Especially if your child receives a significant penalty, is there a process whereby that decision could be reduced or overturned?

Your job in this is not to find a technicality that gets your child off the hook.

Instead, you want to make sure that your child's situation was handled in a professional and equitable manner, and that the school's actions comply with the stated rules and process. If not, you should be contacting the boss of whomever made the disciplinary decision.

Ask Questions

Much like the father did in the story that started this section, it's important to ask good questions when you are contacted by the school about a disciplinary situation.

The point of asking questions isn't to judge whether or not the administrator handled the situation appropriately; quite frankly, it's not your job to supervise how the administrator does her job (but there is advice in the next chapter about what to do if you think the administrator screwed up). Instead, you should ask questions to understand the details of what occurred so that you can take the best steps possible to support and advocate for your child.

In the appendix, there is a list of questions to ask when you hear that your child was involved in a disciplinary situation. In particular, you want to know that:

- Due process occurred.
- There is solid evidence that your child behaved inappropriately (maybe not an open-and-shut case, but solid evidence).

- Your child is being disciplined in accordance with school rules and district policies.
- The school has treated your child professionally and respectfully.

In the story that started the chapter, the father asked some good questions that the administrator was not willing to answer. In some cases, that will happen. Chapter 7 mentioned FERPA and constraints on what administrators can and can't share with a parent. So don't be surprised if an administrator isn't able to tell you everything you might want to know.

Administrators may also not have access to perfect information. Imagine another real-life situation in which a middle school child is hit with a water bottle that someone threw from the top of the stairwell. Despite a thorough investigation, the administrators aren't able to figure out who threw it: there aren't any video cameras at that spot in the building, and there are no witnesses. The student's mother is convinced that someone is targeting her child, and she may be right. But, unfortunately, there just isn't enough information to answer all of her questions or to successfully resolve the situation.

Nevertheless, despite privacy rules and incomplete information, it's not okay for administrators to stonewall a parent. In the story at the start of the chapter, the father suspects that the administrator won't answer some of his questions because he screwed up part of the investigation, and he uses "privacy" as a way to hide that fact.

If you believe an administrator is inappropriately withholding information from you, or choosing not to answer legitimate questions, check out the advice in the next chapter about challenging disciplinary decisions.

SUPPORT YOUR CHILD AND WORK WITH THE SCHOOL

In the wake of a disciplinary situation, one of the most important things for you to do as a parent is to help your child work through what happened, and then put it behind him. The school should be an important partner in helping you do that. Whether it was a minor or major offense, you want to help your child stay positive, stay on track academically, and minimize the chances of getting into trouble again.

Addressing, and Moving Past, the Behavior

There are multiple things you can do to help your child process, and move on from, a school-level disciplinary incident. You may not need to follow all of this advice—it will depend on your child and the situation—but here are the primary steps to consider:

Help your child move forward emotionally—Some students will respond in a healthy and productive way to school-level discipline: they understand what they did wrong, they accept their consequence, and they vow to themselves to never repeat the behavior. Other students have a harder time dealing with the situation. Some may come away sullen and angry that they got into trouble. Still others may be an emotional wreck, suffering a real blow to their self-esteem.

To help your child move forward emotionally, one of the best strategies is to simply listen and commiserate. Have them explain to you in their own language what occurred, and empathize with however they're feeling. Much as was said in the previous chapter on classroom discipline, however, listening is not the same thing as agreeing: you can commiserate with your child's emotions and situation without validating or justifying his behavior.

Consider consequences and incentives at home—It can be perfectly appropriate to put in place consequences at home to match consequences at school. It can also be perfectly appropriate not to impose your own consequences. It really depends on the situation, and what you believe is ultimately best for your child.

For patterns of behavior, however, it can be important for your child to know that continued inappropriate conduct at school will be met with disciplinary action at home. If your child just got into trouble for skipping his third class of the week, it is strongly suggested that you put something in place that penalizes him at home, and that makes it clear that future screw-ups will earn additional consequences.

Similarly, if your child is exhibiting a pattern of behavior and having a hard time breaking it, rewards at home can help. For example, if your middle schooler keeps being referred to the assistant principal for using inappropriate language in class, set up a system such that he earns a reward if he can make it a full week without a referral. After a week or two of success, extend it to two weeks without a referral to earn the reward. (And note, nothing prevents you from using a combination of consequences for bad behavior and incentives for good behavior.)

Be cautious about sharing your misgivings with your child—You may believe that the school absolutely responded in the right way to your child's behavior. In that case, supporting the school's actions is easy. If, however, you think that the administrator went a bit overboard in the consequences, or you're not sure your child is completely guilty, be careful about showing your misgivings to your child.

There is nothing wrong with disagreeing with the school or trying to argue against a consequence; in fact, there is more information on how to do that in the next chapter. But if you make it clear to your child that you don't support the school's actions, you risk a number of negative outcomes. First, you can send your child the signal that her actions were okay, which risks them being repeated. Second, you undermine the authority of the school, which can make your child less likely to respect and follow the rules in the future.

So, how to support the school when you privately disagree? For younger children, commiserate with their feelings, while reinforcing that being at school is kind of like being at home: adults are responsible for making the rules, and adults have to decide how to enforce the rules. For older children, there is a true (if maybe cynical) lesson to be learned: other people aren't perfect, and sometimes life doesn't feel fair.

This can feel like weak tea when your child is complaining about injustice, and you (privately) agree with her. But while it's totally appropriate to share your misgivings with the school administrator, don't let your child know. In the meantime, there's nothing wrong with telling your child, "I know this feels tough, but your life will go on. Let's put this behind you, learn from it, and not get yourself into this sort of situation again."

Ask for help from the school to deal with behaviors—Some parents get freaked out the first time their child gets into trouble. Other parents grow tired of getting repeat calls from the principal when they're just not sure what to do. Either way, school administrators (and their colleagues) are there to help you navigate disciplinary situations: don't be afraid to lean on them for support.

If your child gets into trouble and you're not sure how to handle it, ask the school for advice. While it may be your first time seeing this sort of behavior from your child, the administrator has probably seen it a bunch and has a wealth of experience in how to respond. Guidance counselors, special educators (if your child has an IEP), and ESL teachers (if your child doesn't speak English as his native language) can also be great supports to help you navigate a disciplinary situation with your child. If you want some perspective on the seriousness of your child's behavior, or on ways to keep it from recurring, talk to the administrator who handled the situation and ask for her advice.

If, on the other hand, you have seen a pattern of behavior from your child, and you're just not sure how to stop it, administrators can help with that as well. For especially problematic behaviors, or for a continuing pattern of behavior, administrators might work with parents to put together a behavior contract. This is essentially a document that outlines how the school expects a child to behave (usually targeting a small number of specific behaviors to improve), specific consequences if the behavior continues, potential incentives if the behavior stops, and a plan for how the school will work and communicate with parents in the process. These behavior contracts don't always work, but they are often pretty successful. If you're at the end of your rope with your child's continued troubles at school, ask an administrator if the two of you could work together to put a formalized plan in place to help curb your child's behavior.

Consider social-emotional services for especially concerning stuff—Unfortunately, all too many students experience ongoing issues with substance abuse, sexual behavior, harassing behavior, physical aggression, and so on. Oftentimes, especially when those behaviors are extreme, there are some deep-seated social-emotional or mental health issues underlying the behaviors. When that is the case, a student is likely going to need some formal counseling and support to work through his challenges.

Schools may have specialists on staff who can work with children with more significant social-emotional challenges. These could be guidance counselors, adjustment counselors, social workers, psychologists, and so on. Not every kid qualifies for school-based services, but it sure doesn't hurt to ask. And if a school isn't in a position to provide services from their own staff, they could likely point you in the direction of outside providers. Some schools may even have arrangements with outside counselors to meet with students on campus to make it easier for parents to arrange private counseling.

If your child is exhibiting some extreme behaviors, or if the school brings up the possibility of social-emotional services in the wake of a significant disciplinary situation, it's recommended that you strongly consider this as an option.

Minimizing the Possibility of Academic Ramifications

For a school administrator, it's not uncommon for parents to express concern that their child's disciplinary situation could have an impact on their educational record. In some cases, this concern may be more big-picture, with a worry about how school discipline could reflect on their child's reputation and access to outside institutions (such as colleges or scholarship organizations). In other cases, parents might have more immediate worries: they're concerned that an ISS or OSS could lead to missed work and lower grades.

Chapter 7 spoke in some detail about how discipline plays into a child's overall educational record—please check out that chapter if you have concerns on that front. The short of it is, student disciplinary information is typically kept pretty private, and almost never shared with outside institutions.

Chapter 7 also looked at ISSs and OSSs, and how students are required to be able to make up work that they miss while serving disciplinary consequences. The following information elaborates on those points to help you be more proactive in minimizing the academic ramifications of school discipline.

First of all, this is really only a concern for students who have been assigned some hefty consequences. After-school detention or a lunch spent in the principal's office isn't going to set a student back academically. But one or more days of ISS, or any length of time suspended out of school, can create academic hurdles that aren't always easy to overcome.

Here's advice for ensuring that a more significant disciplinary situation doesn't derail your child's academic progress:

Understand the rules for make-up work—Students who receive an ISS or an OSS should have full make-up privileges. In other words, they have the right to make up any work that is assigned while they are serving their consequence.

While that is a pretty straightforward rule, what can be less straightforward is when that missing work is due. Some teachers may expect the work to be turned in the next day that the student is back in class. Other teachers may be more lenient. The student handbook should have some language around when make-up work is due (logistically, it will probably follow the same rules as those in place for any absence from class). But it would be a good idea to check in with a school administrator to make sure you have a clear sense of the timeline.

An ISS is a little bit easier—after all, your child may actually be able to get a lot of work done since she will be at school for the discipline—but OSSs are trickier, especially suspensions greater than one day. Does a student get a day to complete assignments for every day out? Is there a different timeline for work assigned on the first missed day as opposed to the last one? A good idea would be to send an e-mail to your child's teacher(s), copying the school administrator to make very clear when everything is due.

Find out about missed assignments—Timeline is one piece to the make-up work puzzle, but an even more complicated piece is identifying exactly what work needs to be done. In some cases, this problem may be solved for you. If your child has ISS, there may be someone at the school who organizes missing work and brings it to your child to complete (although don't be surprised if not every assignment makes its way to your child).

OSSs are more complicated. The Internet can be a good friend in staying on top of missing work—many teachers use online tools, such as Google Classroom, to post daily assignments. This makes it relatively easy for a student to log in and see what they missed, assuming they have an Internet connection and computer at home (and if either of those are not the case, let the school know right away—they should be able to help). But if you have a younger child, your child is not particularly organized, or your child's teachers do not post daily assignments online, it can get a little hairy.

In those cases, it is strongly recommended that you send an e-mail to all of your child's teachers asking them to let you know what work needs to be done. Some may respond, "He should know what to do, it's available online," and others may simply say, "I'll check in with him about it when he's back in school." As much as possible, however, you want to help your child get work completed before he returns, rather than waiting until after he's back. The problem is that things can snowball: if he's behind on several assignments when he returns from a suspension, chances are the whole class will be given new work on the day he's back, so now he has an even bigger pile to work through.

Finally, make sure to distinguish between work that *has* to be completed, and work that's discretionary (some teachers may exempt your child from classwork that happened while he was out). Also, make sure you're keeping track of both assignments and assessments. If your child was suspended from school on Tuesday and Wednesday and then is back in school on Thursday, does he need to take that big test on Friday, having missed two days of school? Those are the kinds of details it's helpful to hammer out beforehand.

Stay on top of outstanding work—Figuring out what's due and when it's due are important steps. But many parents think they're done at this point, when they really aren't.

Unfortunately, it's not uncommon to see a kid return from a suspension, have a plan for getting her work done, but then fail to carry through. Instead, the kid struggles with the volume of assignments and ends up just taking zeros on some of them, dropping her grade for the quarter. As the parent, you may know when all of your child's work is due, but she still needs to get it done—and she may need your help following through.

It's recommended that you set up a work schedule with your child, and then monitor her completion of it. It's also recommended that you send a follow-up e-mail to teachers about a week after the discipline has ended, checking to make sure that all of the missed assignments have been completed. This is especially true in high school, where teachers are more likely to expect the child to stay on top of things and less likely to intervene themselves when work is still missing.

Deal comprehensively with longer suspensions—When a child is out of school for an appreciable period of time—really, anything from a week or more—it becomes much more challenging to stay on top of assignments. Part of the issue is coordination. The teachers may expect the child or parent to be coordinating things, the parent may be expecting the school administrator to put together a plan, and the administrator assumes that teachers are on it. The reality is, for a longer suspension, you need to make sure that you, the parent, are actively monitoring your child's work completion.

If your child has an IEP or works with an ESL teacher, those could be great allies to help you stay on top of things. Definitely reach out to them and see if they can serve as your point of contact in the school. Another option at the middle and high school levels is your child's guidance counselor. Just remember, however, that guidance counselors have a range of responsibilities and can easily be assigned 200–300 students, so their bandwidth may be limited in keeping track of your child's progress.

One question to ask of an administrator or guidance counselor is whether or not your child would qualify for tutoring. Sometimes, for longer suspensions, schools will pay for a tutor to work a certain number of hours with a suspended child to help them stay on track.

Another question to ask is about "incompletes." When report cards come out, many schools will offer the option of taking an "incomplete" for students who have missed a significant amount of school, or who were absent for multiple days right as the term ended. An "incomplete" is essentially an extension on getting work done—it means that the grade will not be computed until a later date. Incompletes are usually not open-ended extensions—for example, a school might require that all incompletes be cleaned up within two weeks of the end of the term—but they can provide some breathing room, and they do not have negative ramifications. Once the work gets turned in, your child's grades are then calculated and put into his report card. If your child is suspended near the end of a term, ask an administrator or guidance counselor about the possibility of "incompletes" on the report card to buy your child a little extra time to get work completed.

And one final note about longer suspensions: if your child is facing a long-term suspension in excess of ten days, there are other factors that could come into play. Read on for more information about dealing with especially serious disciplinary situations.

DEALING WITH ESPECIALLY SERIOUS SITUATIONS

In some extreme disciplinary situations, the advice so far just isn't enough. In those cases, you need to consider more significant options.

If your child is going to be out of school for a lengthy period of time—this could be the result of a long-term suspension, or could be a combination of school discipline and legal detention—or if your child is facing the possibility of expulsion, there are three things you need to do:

- Understand the implications fully
- Research the options and resources available
- Explore outside support and/or legal avenues.

Understand the Implications Fully

If your child is involved in a really serious disciplinary situation, you need to understand what all the ramifications might be. Schedule a meeting either with the school principal and/or a guidance counselor. If your child has an IEP or is considered an ELL student, include the staff member in that department who works directly with your child.

In that meeting, you need to ask a bunch of questions. Look in the appendix for a list of questions that cover a variety of possible scenarios.

Research the Options and Resources Available

After speaking with the school, you will want to do some of your own research about the options and resources available. Four big ones to consider are as follows:

- Online learning—Many schools use online learning platforms to educate students who are out of school for extended periods of time. This is especially true at the high school level. The school may proactively talk to you about online learning as an option for your child; if not, definitely bring it up with them. Either way, you will want to do your own research on whatever online content provider(s) the school or district uses.

  In general, online learning tends to be most appropriate when a student is out for forty-five or more days (i.e., a quarter of the year or more). Online learning requires a fair amount of vigilance to make sure a student is getting work done. Your child's school may be able to combine online classes with some district-provided tutoring to help keep your child on track.
- Alternative schools—Some larger districts have their own alternative schools that are available for students with significant suspensions. Smaller districts may partner with a local alternative school that serves a variety of school systems. Before agreeing to have your child placed in an alternative school, try to visit the school to see what the educational environment is like. Some alternative schools have excellent track records of supporting suspended students; others may seem more like a holding area with a heavy focus on behavioral compliance over academic achievement.
- Homeschooling—Different states have different rules when it comes to homeschooling, and many parents may not have the financial or logistical flexibility to be able to homeschool their child. But for some families, the best option for an extended suspension is to formally withdraw your child from school and homeschool them.

  If you choose to do this, make sure you understand exactly what the ramifications of homeschooling will be. Will your child be able to return

to school at some point in the future? How will your child's academic work at home translate to the school's curriculum and expectations? If you are interested in this route, it is strongly advised that you seek out other resources to learn more about this option.
- Switching schools—A final option to consider is simply switching schools. If you have the financial means to do so, switching to a private school could be a possibility. Charter schools might be another option, or looking at schools in a neighboring community (if they allow that possibility).

State laws may mean that a suspension at one public school would need to be served at any public school in the state, so switching schools might not solve the immediate problem. Private schools may not be willing to accept your child as a result of the disciplinary situation (they will likely want full candor from you about why you are leaving your current school), and charter schools may have deadlines around when you can apply. But if you just don't believe that staying at your child's current school is in his best interests, then looking at other options is a good idea.

Explore Outside Support and/or Legal Avenues

Extended suspensions and expulsions are complicated, even for school staff who may have some experience with them. If your child is facing this sort of disciplinary possibility, it's strongly encouraged that you find someone (or someones) who can help you navigate the situation.

In some cases, this might mean hiring an attorney. This can be very expensive, so this is not a step to take lightly. At the same time, attorneys can provide invaluable information and advice throughout a significant disciplinary situation. And, if your child is facing a long-term suspension or expulsion, there's a decent chance that she's facing a legal situation as well: the types of actions that get you long-term suspended or expelled often involve breaking laws.

If you do decide to ask an attorney to help you navigate your child's disciplinary situation, one big piece of advice is to try to find someone who has specific experience with education law. Simply being a lawyer does not make one an expert on the legal complexities of school systems, and some lawyers, because of their lack of knowledge about school systems and education law, can end up not doing a particularly effective job of supporting the students that they're hired to represent.

Having a lawyer doesn't always have to mean paying money out of your own pocket. Depending on your child's situation and the details of the disciplinary incident, it's possible that you may be able to access attorneys that do pro bono work. Especially if you believe that your child's disciplinary situation could be connected in some way to federally defined categories (e.g., race, gender, ethnicity, and sexual orientation), or if there are potential civil rights questions at stake, you might be able to connect with free legal support.

In addition to lawyers, there are a variety of education advocates who work in the K–12 sector. If you're headed to a disciplinary meeting, however, it's not recommended that you just bring along your good friend who happens to also be a teacher in a nearby district—they're not likely to have direct experience with serious disciplinary situations or understand the relevant laws or policies—but professional education advocates could be a real support.

Chapter 10

Your Child Got into Trouble and You Think the School Screwed Up—What Do You Do?

Sometimes, when a principal ends up imposing some pretty stiff consequences on a kid, the parents can go bananas. Principals can end up being called garbage, be told they'll be fired, or be threatened with lawsuits. Far worse, however, are when parents look at a principal and ask—with truly devastated, angry, and desperate looks in their eyes—"How could you *possibly* do this to my child and our family?"

Principals hate those moments. In some situations, the principal might be completely confident that they're making the right decision (although that certainly doesn't change the difficulty of seeing people in real emotional pain). In other situations—in the worst ones—principals second-guess themselves and wonder if they handled things correctly.

Administrators can make mistakes. And, even if they handle a situation by the book, that doesn't reduce the emotional impact on a kid and his parents. If you think an administrator messed up—you think your child is innocent, you think the administrator screwed up the process, or you think that the disciplinary consequences are excessive—there are steps you can take. You may not end up getting the result you're after, but then again, you might. And, if nothing else, you will have provided an administrator, a school, and maybe even a school system with feedback and a perspective that could help them be more effective in the future.

YOU THINK YOUR CHILD IS INNOCENT

When disciplinary situations happen, there are two things that parents can say that always make an administrator wince. First, "My child would never do that." And second, "My child told me she didn't do it, and she never lies to me."

In some of those situations, an administrator has to politely respond, "Well, I'm sorry ma'am, but I am looking at a clear videotape of your child doing exactly that." The fact is, kids are capable of doing all sorts of things that parents would never expect. Remember, children's brains are still developing well into late adolescence. They tend to do things that strike adults as completely boneheaded, but make perfect sense to them. Think back on your own childhood: chances are, you may have done some things back in the day that make you cringe to remember now as an adult, and you would never have admitted those actions to your parents at the time. Well, your kids are growing up in a world in which it is infinitely easier to find trouble, especially via the electronic devices that they are so addicted to.

A school administrator may tell you that your kid did something, and you simply can't believe it's true. You may even be right. But—having seen plenty of parents' eyes expand as they watched the video of their child doing exactly that—please allow for the possibility that you may also be wrong.

Nevertheless, simply asserting your child's innocence won't be enough to get them off. Keep reading to find out how to more substantively challenge a disciplinary decision.

YOU THINK THE SCHOOL SCREWED UP THE PROCESS

If you believe that the school screwed up the process while handling your child's disciplinary situation, there are some specific steps you can take. But first here is some more general advice:

- Figure out where you stand on your child's guilt—Before you take steps to challenge a disciplinary decision, be very honest with yourself about your child's guilt. Do you truly believe that your child is innocent? If your real motive for challenging the disciplinary decision is that you want to keep your kid out of trouble—in other words, you think he may very well have done what he was accused of doing, but you just don't want to see him serve the consequences—you're on shaky ground. It's admirable to want to defend your child, but you're strongly cautioned against doing so when you think he's probably guilty.
- Find out if there is a formal appeals opportunity—For lengthy out-of-school suspensions (OSSs), especially those in excess of ten days, there may be a formal appeals process. Even if there is not a formal process in place, there may be an informal opportunity to plead your case (e.g., if an assistant principal made the disciplinary decision, you could speak with

the principal). The Student Handbook, which was discussed in the previous chapter, should have information about how to request an appeal.
- Don't let principle overcome pragmatism—When a student and her parents get really worked up over a relatively minor disciplinary situation, it can be hard to understand why. There are times when it's worth it to fight for principle—you know your child is innocent, despite what the school contends—but an after-school detention is probably not that time.
- Remember that, ultimately, the school gets to make the call—The previous chapter mentioned that school administrators are essentially the judge, jury, and executioner when it comes to school discipline. Like it or not, the school almost always gets to make the final call about disciplinary situations. That's not an argument against advocating for your child, just a dose of realism for you to keep in mind during the process.

Having reviewed that general advice, let's now turn to some specific instances in which you might challenge a disciplinary situation on procedural grounds and look at suggestions about how to handle them. As a general rule, there are three ways in which a school can screw up a disciplinary process. First, they can handle the situation by the book, but treat students and/or parents in an inappropriate manner in the process. Second, they can lack sufficient evidence to impose a consequence. And third, they can fail to follow their own procedural rules and policies. Let's look at each one of these.

You Accept the Disciplinary Outcome, but Don't Like the Way You or Your Child Was Treated

Throughout a disciplinary situation, your child should be treated professionally, respectfully, and as an individual; you should be treated professionally and as a partner; the situation should be handled privately and discreetly; and there should be no lasting repercussions for you or your child after the disciplinary situation is resolved (e.g., administrators or teachers shouldn't continue to bring up the situation with you or your child in future conversations).

If this is not the case, there are a couple steps that you should take. First, you should let the offending party know about your concerns. This could happen via e-mail, but would preferably happen through a phone call or face-to-face conversation. In that conversation, be polite but honest, and give the other person the opportunity to explain himself or, potentially, apologize.

If your concern is significant enough, let the person's boss know. For an assistant principal, the boss would be the principal. For a principal, the boss would be the superintendent or, in a larger school district, a regional superintendent.

If you are concerned about how your child might be treated going forward, make some specific requests about your future expectations. For example, if an assistant principal yelled at your child, make it clear that you do not want school staff to raise their voice to your child in the future. For these sorts of requests, it is strongly recommended that you put them in writing to create a paper trail (that could be in a follow-up e-mail after speaking with the person).

Finally, if you have real concerns about the administrator's ability to treat your child or you appropriately in the future, you can request that another administrator be assigned to work with your child. This request may not be honored—and you shouldn't make it lightly—but there are times when a different administrator would simply be a better fit for your kid.

You Don't Think There Is Sufficient Evidence to Justify a Consequence

In some cases, an administrator may make a decision to punish a student even when the evidence isn't airtight. The administrators are convinced that the student has committed the offense, but there's some ambiguity in the evidence. If that happens to your child—they receive consequences with some shaky justification—it's perfectly appropriate to ask questions, to push back, and even to flat-out disagree.

Remember, however, that there is a difference between "My kid probably did it, but I don't think the school can prove it" and "It really doesn't seem like my kid did it." You're strongly encouraged not to try to get your kid off on a technicality. It's very important that kids understand that actions have consequences, and that "they weren't able to catch me" is not a good justification for inappropriate behavior.

Another thing to remember is that schools aren't like courts of law. In a court you are innocent until proven guilty, and the onus of responsibility is on the prosecutor to prove that you did something. Now, the assumption shouldn't be that students are guilty until proven innocent, but school administrators get to decide when they believe they have enough evidence to impose consequences. So just because you disagree with a decision doesn't mean that you have the power to change it.

That having been said, if you believe your child is innocent and there is insufficient evidence to justify a consequence, make your case to the administrator handling the situation. And if you're dealing with an assistant principal and you feel strongly enough, make an appointment to speak with the principal and explain your concerns. The principal may very well support her assistant principal—it's not good for organizational moral if staff believe that their decisions will regularly be overturned anytime a parent complains—but it doesn't hurt to make the argument.

You Believe the School Failed to Follow Its Own Procedural Rules

This is the area in which a disciplinary situation is most likely to go off the rails. Schools are busy places, and administrators have big jobs that can keep them running all day. Sometimes, in the rush to resolve a disciplinary situation, an administrator can cut corners. In other situations, administrators make assumptions that don't pan out, initially accusing a child of inappropriate behavior only to find out later that the kid was innocent. And in some situations, administrators just screw up and don't handle things well.

In the previous chapter, you were advised to read the Student Handbook and ask questions of administrators in a disciplinary situation. For the purposes here, the assumption is that you've already done that. Next, match the rules to what you learn about the situation. Did the administrator follow due process? If someone searched your child, was it handled in accordance with district policies? Did a police officer question your child without your permission? Did the administrator interview any student witnesses? Does the school have video cameras, and if so, was that information reviewed (a brief side note: you may be able to request to see video camera footage of your child, so long as other children are not also shown or identified in the same footage)? Does the Student Handbook identify mandatory limits to disciplinary consequences for your child's behavior? Did the administrator ignore additional evidence that might have exonerated your child? Again, your goal isn't to find some technicality that gets your kid off the hook, but rather to make sure that your child's situation was handled appropriately.

If you do see inconsistencies in the way a situation was handled, please stay reasonable. There are often minor discrepancies in any disciplinary situation, and what your child tells you will likely not reconcile 100 percent with what an administrator tells you. But if you see real procedural problems that impacted the situation—an administrator closed his office door and then got in your child's face, yelling at him to admit to the behavior—that is truly problematic.

In that case, you need to share your concerns with the administrator who handled the situation. Be polite, but be direct. If the administrator becomes defensive or refuses to at least listen to you or consider your concerns, contact his boss (the principal, if you met with an assistant principal; the principal's boss, if you met with the principal) to schedule a time to meet. In that meeting, be sure to provide as factual and unemotional a summary of what occurred as possible, along with your specific concerns. Bring along a copy of the Student Handbook or relevant district policies and point out the pertinent ones in the meeting.

Here's another real-life story with a "please don't do this" piece of advice. A principal is working on a complex disciplinary situation that involves a large group of kids, and one of the parents disagrees with the way it's being handled. So, the parent ends up confronting a number of students involved in the situation—she does this outside of school—and essentially conducts her own investigation. She then comes to the principal with the results, telling him that what she's learned contradicts the principal's decisions.

While one can certainly understand the frustration with thinking that a school administrator hasn't handled a situation well, please avoid the temptation to insert yourself into the middle of things and investigate the details on your own. It will almost certainly not help your child's case, and you will likely make matters worse in the process, potentially ticking off other kids' parents.

YOU THINK THE CONSEQUENCES ARE EXCESSIVE

You may not have procedural concerns per se with the way your child's disciplinary situation was handled, but you believe your child's punishment is simply too much. In that case, here are multiple pieces of advice.

Ask the Administrator to Explain the Consequence

Especially if this is the first time your child has gotten into trouble at this level, you may have no real sense of what a consequence could or should be. So, ask the administrator to explain why she picked what she did. The goal of this question shouldn't be accusatory—and you're not asking the administrator to justify her decision—you simply want to understand why the school is imposing this consequence for this behavior. After hearing the explanation, you may change your mind and agree that the consequence does seem reasonable. Or you may not. But either way, you'll have a better sense of the reasons underlying it.

Check the Student Handbook

If you're at work or at home and get "the call" from an administrator, you're probably not going to be in a position to say, "Hold on, I need to go check my parent advice book and see what Parry says to do about this situation." Chances are you'll be caught off-guard, your mind will be trying to process a thousand thoughts at once, and some strong emotions (shock, frustration, disappointment) will kick in that will limit your ability to think clearly.

That's all okay. After the call has ended and you have the time to do so, get a copy of the Student Handbook (from your child or from the school's website) and double-check to see if it says anything about your child's actions and related consequences. Make sure that the administrator's decision is in keeping with the school's practices. If it isn't, call the administrator back and politely point this out. And even if the Handbook says your child's punishment is reasonable (or if it doesn't say one way or the other), you can still call the administrator back and ask about flexibility. Which leads to the next piece of advice . . .

Just Ask the Administrator If the Punishment Can be Lessened

Here's another real-life story: A mother who's an actual judge meets with her son's principal to try to convince him to reduce her son's ISS to a lesser punishment. She's incredibly polite and professional, but the irony is not lost on the principal when she asks him to consider "mercy" for her kid.

Much like the judge, you can always just ask an administrator to reduce a punishment.

In some situations, an administrator may not have much wiggle room and wants to treat your child consistently with the way she has treated other children in the past. But administrators often have discretion. It's not uncommon for an administrator to call a parent, explain what their child has done, and then say, "Here's what I'm thinking about doing, does that seem reasonable to you?" In other instances, an administrator may tell a parent, "I'm giving your child a day of in-school-suspension," and the parent pushes back: "My son has been struggling academically recently and I hate to see him miss a day of classes—is there something else we could do?" In those situations, an administrator might be willing to be flexible.

If you do want to ask for a punishment to be lessened, have a good argument for why. It could be that this is your child's first time getting into trouble. It could be that your child has been going through a difficult time outside of school. It could be that your child is struggling academically (like the example above) and you want to prioritize having your child in class. If the administrator says that she can't be flexible, then she can't. But there's no harm in asking.

Appeal Informally

If you asked about having a punishment lessened and got "No" for an answer, and you still feel that the consequence is egregious, you can always get in touch with the next person on the org chart. This is easier to do if the person handling the situation was an assistant principal and you can appeal to the principal (superintendents generally will not get involved in school-level discipline unless a really significant consequence has been handed out).

There are certainly times when parents might contact a principal to appeal a decision made by an assistant principal. More often than not, a principal is likely to support the other administrator's decision. But sometimes, behind the scenes, the assistant principal might go to the principal and say, "Look, I took a pretty hard line on this situation, but it won't bother me at all if you want to lessen things a bit." Principals don't generally like to undermine their assistant principals' authority, but there are times when they will be willing to reduce a consequence.

Appeal Formally

For really serious consequences (typically an OSS in excess of ten days), there will likely be a formal appeals process. If you think your child's punishment is excessive, take advantage of that opportunity. There might even be some situations in which a principal advises parents to appeal. For example, if district policies don't give the principal any flexibility or discretion, but the principal doesn't necessarily agree with the policy's outcome, they might encourage parents to appeal the ruling and get the penalty reduced.

Chapter 11

Your Child Is a Victim—What Do You Do?

The assumption in the previous chapters has been, "Your child did something he shouldn't." But what if your child didn't do anything wrong? What if your child is the victim?

The final chapter of this section talks in detail about how to handle situations when your child is the victim of someone else's behavior. The first part looks at situations in which another student has treated your child inappropriately, but the school isn't aware. The second part talks about how to handle circumstances in which your child is the victim of a disciplinary situation involving another student, and the school either already has or is in the process of investigating the situation. And finally, the third part looks at one of the most difficult and concerning possibilities: your child is the victim of a school staff member's behavior.

YOUR CHILD IS A VICTIM OF ANOTHER STUDENT'S BEHAVIOR, AND THE SCHOOL IS UNAWARE

Unfortunately, just about any child can be the subject of another student's inappropriate behavior. Also, unfortunately, kids are pretty good at being mean to each other without the school ever finding out. If your child ends up in this situation—another child is treating him inappropriately, and no one at the school is aware of it—there are a number of steps for you to take. First, you want to understand the details of the situation. Next, if you think it's appropriate, you should contact the school to make them aware. If the situation warrants it, you should then work with the school to come up with a plan to address the situation. Finally, you should continue to check on your child to make sure the plan is working.

Understand the Situation

Once you become aware that your child is a victim of another student's behavior, your first step is to understand the details of the situation. Your best source of information is, of course, your child. Younger children may have a difficult time providing an objective accounting of what's going on, and older children may be disinclined to share too much (middle schoolers and high schoolers are notorious for thinking they can handle situations on their own, and for wanting to keep their parents out of their private lives). Nevertheless, see if you can get as much of the story as possible from your child.

If you believe that you're only getting part of the story, consider some other information-gathering options. If you have another child at the same school (especially an older child), they might have information. Depending on the situation, the parents of other children in your child's class or grade may know something as well. Finally, if your child is older and has an electronic device (cell phone, tablet, laptop, etc.), and the situation involves interactions with another child, see if there are any electronic messages (text messages, direct messages, chats, photos, etc.) between your child and the other child(ren).

As you do all this, you're trying to accomplish three things:

- Determine the objective severity of the situation—In many circumstances, children become upset over situations that are just not objectively that serious. Another child made fun of them during lunch, another member of the football team criticized their athletic skills, or their best friend wouldn't play with them at recess. In other circumstances, however, children can be the victim of truly inappropriate behavior: threats, bullying or harassment, physical or sexual assault, and so on. If the situation gets your Spidey-sense tingling, you should take it seriously.
- Determine the severity of the situation through your child's eyes—Sometimes, a situation that we as adults would view as pretty benign can feel truly devastating to a kid. Alternatively, situations that might shock us can seem commonplace to kids. In addition to determining the objective severity of the situation, figure out what it means to your kid. This will help you in deciding how to respond.
- Decide whether or not it's worth contacting the school—If you think a situation is serious—or even if it doesn't seem serious to you, but it appears to be having a real negative impact on your child—it's strongly recommended that you reach out to the school to help address it. On the other hand, if you and your child agree that a situation is not serious, or you think your child is over-reacting, you could certainly consider coaching your child through

it yourself. Finally, if you think a situation is serious—for example, your child has been getting semi-threatening text messages from another kid for the last couple weeks—but your child claims it's not a big deal, trust *your* instincts, not your child's, and reach out to the school.

If you do decide to contact the school, just keep one thing in the back of your mind: you probably don't yet have the full story. It's not uncommon for an administrator to hear from a concerned parent about how their child is being treated by another student, only to have the reality turn out to be a little bit more complicated. Yes, another student is treating their child inappropriately, but it turns out *their* child initiated the situation with some inappropriate behavior of their own.

This doesn't mean you shouldn't trust your child, and it certainly doesn't mean that all student victims turn out to be guilty themselves. In fact, far from it: there are plenty of situations in which one student is clearly a victim and has done nothing wrong. But if you do reach out to the school, just don't be surprised if it ultimately turns out that your child hasn't been completely innocent himself (and just to be clear, that's not an argument against contacting the school—if your child is a victim of worrisome behavior, it's important to do something to address it).

Talk to the School

When you contact the school, there are two important points to consider: who to contact and how to frame the concern. The following information will walk you through each of those points.

First of all, who to contact. If your child is a victim of classroom-based behavior, and the behavior is not super-serious—for example, another student is teasing your child on the playground or in class—your best bet is to get in touch with the classroom teacher. By "classroom-based behavior," this means behavior at recess with classmates, or behavior in the halls or cafeteria when part of a specific class.

If, however, the behavior is more serious, the behavior extends across multiple classes (for middle or high school students), or the behavior is taking place in other areas of the building (e.g., before school or on the bus), your best bet is to contact an administrator, starting with an assistant principal (if your school has one). You could certainly reach out to a classroom teacher for advice on how to handle it, but more serious behaviors, and behaviors that happen in common spaces outside the purview of a teacher, are really administrators' domain. If the behavior is related to a social conflict—for example, another student is teasing your child—you could contact a guidance counselor for advice. But an assistant principal is a good default contact.

The next point to consider is how you want to frame the concern. Is this a "Just want to let you know," an "I need your help with this," or an "I need you to investigate and do something quickly" situation?

The first category—"Just want you to know"—represents a less-serious situation. Maybe another student has been calling your child names at recess, and you want to make sure the teacher is aware. You believe your child can deal with the situation independently and you're not asking the teacher to take any specific steps, you just want the situation on the teacher's radar. If this is a "Just want you to know" situation, reach out to the teacher (e-mail or a phone call would be best), explain the details as factually as possible, and make it explicitly clear that you're not asking for any specific steps to be taken.

The second category—"I need your help with this"—means you're looking for some action on the part of the school. That could simply be advice: you aren't sure if this is something to worry about or not, and you want the teacher or administrator to advise you on what should happen next. In other situations, you're looking for some sort of intervention on the school's part to help end the situation. Make sure you share the details of what you know (e-mail, phone call, or face-to-face are all fine), and be clear that you're looking for some sort of help from the school.

The final category—"I need you to investigate and do something quickly"—is for more serious situations that have you truly worried. For this level of concern, reach out to an administrator. You could do it via e-mail, but a phone call or face-to-face meeting would be best. When you speak to the administrator, share the details of what you know. If there is any electronic evidence—text messages, online messages, and so on—bring copies of those as well. Make it clear that you need the situation to be addressed quickly.

One final note: before contacting the school, decide whether or not you're going to inform your child of what you're doing. For younger children, it's strongly recommended that you don't tell them of your plan—what you don't want is your child going to school the next day and bragging to the other kids that "My mom called the teacher and got Johnny in trouble!" If your younger child is particularly anxious about the situation, you could say a simple, "Let me contact the school and try to fix this for you." For older children, it's really up to you to decide how to handle informing your child. Some kids will push back if they think you'll contact the school, whereas others won't mind. Definitely don't say something like, "I'm going to call the school right now and get that kid suspended!" But if you think it's appropriate, let your child know that you're planning to take some action.

Come Up with a Plan

If you're looking for some sort of action on the school's part, that means that there needs to be a plan put in place: either after you have the conversation with the teacher or administrator, or after the person you meet with has had an opportunity to investigate the concern.

A plan doesn't have to be something formally written down or complex. It could be as simple as the teacher promising, "I'm going to make sure I keep your child separated from the other student during class activities, and I'll carefully monitor their behavior at recess." Schools have a variety of steps they can take to address situations between students: mediation with the help of an adult, separating students from each other in class or in their class schedules, verbal warnings, disciplinary consequences, formal behavior plans, and so on.

When you speak with the teacher or administrator, be open to their suggestions about the best way to handle the situation. Chances are they have dealt with similar situations in the past and have a pretty good sense of what will work. Be sure to give your input and opinions about the plan, but you are strongly advised against going in with a specific set of expectations in mind.

Once a plan is in place, you want to make sure there is clarity on three points:

- The details of the plan—Make sure you fully understand what is going to happen. It's recommended that you send a follow-up e-mail to the teacher or administrator, thanking them for their help, and reiterating your understanding of what is going to occur. At the end of the e-mail, say something to the effect of, "If there is anything that I have missed or misunderstood, please let me know."
- The next communication steps—As part of the plan, have an agreed next step for communication. Is the teacher going to send you an e-mail after a week to let you know what he's seeing? Is the administrator going to call you back the next day to confirm that the plan is in place? Are you going to meet with the administrator again at some point to review how things are going? Make sure you formally decide with the teacher or administrator when the next follow-up communication is going to take place and who's responsible for initiating it.
- The involvement of your child—Make sure that both you and the teacher (or administrator) are clear on how your child will be involved. Is the teacher going to mediate a conversation between your child and another student? Is your child going to be kept in the dark about what's happening? Is the administrator going to initiate a conversation with your child to explain the steps the school is taking? What you don't want is for your child

to find out about your efforts when you thought everything would be kept under wraps, especially if your child is a teenager that doesn't like having his parents meddle in his affairs.

Monitor the Plan's Effectiveness

After a plan is put in place, you want to know if it's working. There should already be an agreement about when you and the teacher or administrator will follow up, but make sure that things don't end there. Consider checking back in after several weeks to see how things are going. If your child is aware of the plan, make sure you're checking in with him about how things are going. Be careful not to hover—if you ask your child first thing at the end of each day, "Were things better today?", that might keep the situation going in your child's mind rather than helping your child to move past it.

Don't be surprised if things don't go exactly as planned. Sometimes a parent is concerned about how another student is treating his child, the administrator puts in place a plan to keep them separated, and a couple days later the kids are happily eating lunch together in the cafeteria. In some extreme situations two kids might get into a fight, the school changes their schedules to keep them separated, and they end up being best friends by the end of the year. That's not to minimize situations in which a child is a victim—more often than not, kids who are separated stay separated and want no more to do with each other—but simply to point out that children's relationships can be fluid. You can bend over backward to protect your kid, only to see them completely undermine your efforts by gravitating back toward the child who had victimized them. That's not an argument for parents not to go to bat for their kids; instead, it's an argument for keeping tabs on how things progress after a situation has been addressed.

Final Thoughts

Here's another story: A parent's elementary school daughter is being teased by another student on the bus. The parent gets so fed up that she walks onto the bus one day and confronts the other child: "Leave my daughter alone!"

Needless to say, that doesn't go over so well. The other child's parents are understandably upset, and the first parent has to meet with the school principal, who politely reminds her that accosting other children on school property (which school buses are considered to be) is not okay.

This story introduces a couple final thoughts.

The first, which relates directly to the parent's situation, is *don't take matters into your own hands*. When parents insert themselves into school disciplinary situations, it pretty much never ends well. In the parent's situation in the story, she changes the focus from what's happening to her child—getting teased on the bus—to what she does to someone else's child. As much as you might want to protect your kid, work *with* the school. Beware the ramifications of trying to solve the problem yourself.

Another, unrelated final thought: *be careful about feeding your child's proclivity for drama.* If every dinner-table conversation turns into, "So, what did Sarah say to you *today* at school?", chances are your child is going to enjoy the attention and keep the drama going. This isn't to say that you can't talk to your child about a difficult situation—of course, you can and should do that—but be careful to keep your focus on solving problems rather than perpetuating them.

And one final thought: *as much as schools can help, sometimes you need to escalate to protect your child.* This thought relates to more serious situations, especially those in which you are concerned about your child's physical safety. If your child has been threatened, has been physically or sexually assaulted, or is the subject of repeated harassment, you may want to speak with the police as well as the school. Unfortunately, sometimes it takes the threat of legal action to get a kid to end their behavior. If your child's school has a School Resource Officer, talk with her about your options. And if the school doesn't have an SRO, don't hesitate to ask the school to put you in touch with the police or to go to the police station yourself.

YOUR CHILD IS A VICTIM OF ANOTHER STUDENT'S BEHAVIOR IN A SCHOOL-INVESTIGATED SITUATION

So far this chapter has looked at what to do if your child is a victim of another child's behavior and the school was unaware of the situation. Now the focus will switch to how to react when your child is a victim and the school is already actively involved in addressing the situation.

This could be something minor: the teacher observed another student speaking to your child inappropriately, and the teacher's just calling to let you know about how the situation has been handled. It could also be something major: your child was the victim of another student's sexually harassing behavior.

The steps for you to take are similar to the ones you would take if the school had not been aware of the situation, with a couple extra wrinkles.

Understand What Happened from the School's Perspective

Similar to the advice given in earlier pages, you want to understand what happened. When you first get a call from the school explaining the situation, especially if the situation is more serious, you may be caught off-guard. In that case, don't hesitate to call the school back for more information after you've collected yourself and processed what occurred. You may also want to contact the school after you've had a chance to speak to your child (which can prompt new questions, especially if your child's account of the situation differs from the school's). Some important points to consider:

- Take notes while talking to the school—For a minor situation, this may not be as necessary. But for more complicated or serious situations, it's important to have an objective collection of notes that you can use when speaking to your child, your significant other, or when following up with the school.
- Check on your child's current physical and emotional health—If the school is letting you know about a minor situation that has already been resolved, this may not be that important. But even for minor circumstances, it doesn't hurt to ask, "How did my child seem to you after the situation was over?" For more serious situations—for example, if your child was physically assaulted by another student—you may want to speak to your child right away to see if they need to come home.
- Remember that the school has privacy obligations—As discussed in chapter 6, schools cannot share information that relates to another student's educational record. So, the school might not be able to give you other students' names or describe anything about other students' past behaviors (there can be some exceptions to this based on state or local law—Title IX investigations are one example).

Understand What Happened from Your Child's Perspective

Make sure you take time to speak with your child to understand what happened from his perspective. It's recommended that you allow your child to tell his story without specific prompting on your part. For example, avoid saying things such as, "The assistant principal told me that the other student said something to you, is that true?" This way you are more likely to get a truer understanding of how the situation felt to your child.

When your child tells his story, there may be some discrepancies between what he relates and what the school related. This could be due to a variety of factors, most of them not nefarious. But it's also possible that your child has information that the school doesn't have, that your child is choosing not to share with you everything that he knows, or that the school has missed something or made a mistake in the process. Minor discrepancies between the stories are probably ignorable; major discrepancies are worth following up on with the school.

Understand How the School Has Addressed the Situation

After you understand what happened, you want to know how the school is dealing with it. It's possible that the situation is minor and requires minimal action on the school's part. But, if the situation is more serious, there are a number of topics to speak to the school about:

- Is the investigation concluded, or is it still ongoing? In many cases, the school will contact you after a situation has been completely resolved. In other cases, they may still be in the process of investigating what occurred, but they know your child is a victim and want to let you know. If the investigation is still ongoing, ask for information about the timeline for concluding it and for the next steps that the school plans to take. For example, do they still need to speak with other student witnesses? Do they need your child's cooperation in some way? If they don't know who committed the act (e.g., if your child received an anonymous threat or had money stolen from her locker), how likely are they to figure it out?
- Is there a possibility that your child acted inappropriately? As was mentioned earlier in this chapter, it's possible for a student to be both a victim and a perpetrator. For example, maybe another student has been harassing your child for weeks, and your child finally pushed him in the hall. Make sure you ask the school if they have any reason to believe that your child is culpable in some way.
- How will your child be kept safe going forward? Especially if your child was the victim of more serious behavior, ask the school about their plan to ensure your child's safety. Look back at the previous section's discussion of developing a plan for a student victim for more details.
- Are there consequences for the other student(s)? If the school has determined that another student (or other students) has acted inappropriately toward your child, ask the school about consequences for the other student(s). The school probably can't give you specifics because of privacy laws—they can't say, "We're putting that student into in-school suspension for two days"—but they can give you a sense of how similar actions are typically handled.

Keep in Touch with Your Child and the School about How Things Are Going

If the disciplinary situation involving your child has been resolved, that doesn't necessarily mean that it's "over." Make sure that you check in with your child occasionally about how things are going (while still allowing your child to move forward from the situation). Also make sure that you follow up with the school after a week or so to see if they are seeing any lingering issues. If a specific plan was put in place related to your child's safety, check to make sure that the plan is being followed and that it's working.

If the disciplinary situation involving your child is still being investigated, make clear to the school (most likely an assistant principal or principal) that you would like to be kept in the loop. School administrators have a lot on their plates, and it is easy for their focus to shift to whatever the next situation or challenge might be. Don't be afraid to reach out and politely remind the school if you haven't heard from them and are wondering where things stand. Especially if your child was the subject of a more serious disciplinary situation, make sure you're advocating with the school to keep your child safe while they finish the investigation.

Consider If You Need to Take More Extreme Measures to Keep Your Child Safe

As was true in the previous section, there may be times when you need to turn to outside agencies, most notably the police, to ensure your child's safety. In some cases, the school may even encourage you to do so. If the situation involving your child was a serious one, and your child was not just the victim of a school rule violation but also a legal violation, don't hesitate to speak with a police officer.

YOUR CHILD IS THE VICTIM OF A SCHOOL STAFF MEMBER'S BEHAVIOR

Unfortunately, these sorts of situations can happen in schools, and they are incredibly challenging. In some circumstances, a school may be able to work through it and repair the relationship. In other circumstances—especially if a teacher has acted in a physically aggressive manner toward a student—the teacher will end up being let go from the school.

From a process standpoint, you'll want to do the same sorts of things as in the preceding sections of this chapter in which your child might be a victim. Specifically:

- Understand the details of the situation
- Understand how your child views the situation
- Talk to the school (if they haven't already contacted you)
- Understand the school's plan to address the situation
- Monitor the success of the plan

But there are some details that make this different from a situation in which your child is the victim of another student's behavior. Specifically, this section will walk you through the definition of what "inappropriate" staff behavior looks like, especially given the power relationship between staff and students and given the role that staff members play as authority figures. It also discusses what a school's response plan might be. And finally, this section concludes by discussing the role that the police might play when inappropriate staff behavior has occurred.

Defining "Inappropriate" Staff Behavior

Some staff behavior toward students is clearly inappropriate. If a staff member makes sexual comments or touches your child in a sexually suggestive way; if a staff member is aggressive toward your child, making threats or physical contact in an aggressive manner; or if a staff member belittles your child because of her physical appearance, race, ethnicity, religion, gender, sexual orientation, or some other protected category, there's really no nuance: the staff member has clearly been inappropriate.

In other situations, however, the definition of "inappropriate" can be vague. High school coaches can sometimes use colorful language and may get in a student's face with a raised voice. In the classroom, some teachers can be pretty strict, while others employ sarcastic humor that rubs students the wrong way. In a dangerous situation, a teacher may put his hands on a student to prevent a fight. In other situations, a teacher may make an insensitive comment toward a student who keeps pushing his buttons.

The point is that, in some circumstances, what feels inappropriate to one parent might feel perfectly appropriate to another. You might think your child's history teacher has high standards and gets the best out of your kid, while your neighbor thinks the teacher pushes kids too hard and damages their self-esteem.

If you're on the fence—you're not entirely comfortable with the way a staff member is treating your child, but it's not an obvious case of inappropriate behavior—you should reach out to a school staff member whom you trust. This could be a teacher, but know that teachers often feel awkward being given negative information and being asked for advice about their colleagues. Instead, the best recommendation would be a guidance counselor or an administrator. When you talk to them, describe the situation as objectively as you can and ask them for advice. Does the behavior sound inappropriate? Should you reach out directly to speak with the teacher about it? Should you ignore it? Should you formally report it?

As professionals and people in a position of trust, school staff members are responsible for treating students with respect, care, and dignity, and it's not okay when they fail to do so. At the same time, as authority figures responsible for maintaining safety and distraction-free learning environments, school staff have some latitude in the way that they need to act with an energetic group of kids in front of them for 180 days a year.

Good teachers don't always teach or act exactly the way parents think they should, and that's okay. But inappropriate behavior, even from the best teacher (or administrator, or other staff member), is not okay. When in doubt, check in with the school.

The Details of a Plan to Address the Inappropriate Staff Behavior

If a staff member has treated your child inappropriately, there are two important details to any follow-up plan that need to be explicitly explained: how will contact between your child and the staff member be handled going forward and what is happening to the staff member as a result of the situation.

In less-serious situations—maybe a teacher blew up at your child in class, but never made any threatening comments and didn't use any over-the-top language—your child and the teacher may be able to resolve the situation and move forward without any big changes (other than an apology and agreement on how to prevent the situation from happening again). For more serious circumstances, however—a teacher put her hands on your child or made a sexually inappropriate comment—you may want to know that your child will be removed from the class, without penalty, and that the staff member will not have any more contact with her (assuming, of course, that they have not been fired as a result).

Whatever the details turn out to be, make sure that you (and your child, if appropriate) have a clear understanding of what the relationship with the staff member will be like going forward. Can the teacher say "Hi" to her in the hall if they happen to pass each other, or should there be no contact? If the staff member is going to be out of the building for a period of time, will the teacher be back in class with your child when he returns? Is your child allowed to reach out to the teacher, or should your child avoid initiating any contact? Make sure that everyone—you, the school administrator, your child—are all on the same page as to the plan going forward.

In addition to knowing how contact will be handled, you'll also want to know what is happening to the staff member. On this point, there is only so much information that the school can share. For example, if the teacher is receiving a negative evaluation as a result of the situation, that's personnel information that the school can't tell you about. But the school *can* give you some general information. For example, an administrator might tell a parent, in response to a complaint, "We are going to be conducting a formal human resources investigation of this incident. I can't let you know what the outcome of that investigation is, but please know that this is being done formally in collaboration with our Director of HR."

So, don't expect that a school will keep you apprised of the details of how the situation is handled. But the school absolutely can give you a sense of how seriously they view the situation, steps that they are taking to resolve it, and what some possible ramifications might be.

Involving the Police and/or Courts

Here's an unfortunate real-life situation: A substitute teacher in an elementary school puts his hands on a child inappropriately during recess, and an administrator witnesses the situation. After conducting an investigation with the help of Human Resources, the principal makes the decision to no longer allow the person to work at the school. When the principal speaks to the parent about what happened, the principal also makes it clear that, if the parent thinks it's appropriate, she might want to reach out to the police. And because the school no longer has a relationship with the staff member, the parent's decision to do so won't have any impact on the school.

Much as you were advised in earlier sections in this chapter, you should consider speaking with the police if your child has been treated in a potentially criminal manner. But if you take legal action against a staff member who is still employed by the school, especially if you see the situation as more significant than the school views it, things can get complicated. That is not an argument against involving the police or against seeking legal representation; instead, just a caution to keep a couple things in mind as the process unfolds.

First, make it very clear to the school that you want no contact whatsoever between the staff member and your child while the legal process plays out. Next, make it clear that you expect there to be no negative ramifications for your child as a result of your legal actions: no comments from other teachers to your child, no academic or extracurricular penalties, and so on. Finally, it's strongly recommended that you keep your child as far out of the process as possible. You want your child to be able to go on with his normal life at school while the process plays out, and that means shielding him as much as possible from the actions you're taking.

In more serious situations, chances are that the school will be taking its own personnel actions toward the staff member, and these actions will work in parallel to any legal proceedings. In fact, it is very likely that by the time a case gets to court, the staff member will have become an ex-staff member. Either way, however, make sure you have a clear understanding of how your child will be treated at school in the meantime.

Section 3

PARENT INVOLVEMENT

WHY PARENTS ARE A SCHOOL'S QUALITY CONTROL

Talk to any high school principal and they will tell you that one of their favorite events is the prom. Getting to see the kids all dressed up and having fun on the dance floor is an absolute joy.

But as the evening comes to an end, those principals will start to stress out. A common tradition in many high schools in America is for kids to head to parties after the prom, and those parties sometimes include drinking and drug use. Principals worry every year that they'll be woken up with a phone call in the middle of the night, informing them that a student has been involved in an accident.

To try and address these worries, many high schools have something in place called an "After Prom," a party that takes place immediately after the prom and is typically sponsored by the school and hosted by parents. The idea of these sorts of parties is to have a fun, substance-free place where kids can hang out and socialize late into the night.

So, here's a real-life story: A high school where the After Prom isn't very popular. Administrators struggle every year to get kids to attend and to convince parents that they shouldn't allow private parties at their homes. But all to no avail: After Prom attendance remains low, and tons of kids go to private parties.

Until, one year, it all changes.

At one of those private parties after the prom, a group of students end up having to go to the hospital. A lot of parents in town find out about it, and it really spooks them. It's especially scary for the parents of kids who will be old enough to go to the prom the following year. So, the parents decide to do something about it.

They create a new planning committee and go on a fund-raising spree, tripling the amount of money typically spent on the After Prom. They start guilting their friends and get parents throughout the community to agree to not let kids host their own parties. And then they put together a fantastic After Prom party, dramatically increasing the number of student attendees.

Now, to be fair, a lot of kids go to the After Prom under duress that year. Their parents tell them it's either that or be home at an early hour. But, once the students are there, they have a great time. And just like that the culture and tradition changes. The next year, a new group of parents builds on the success of the previous year, hosting another great After Prom, and most students come to it. With each successive year, it becomes that much easier to keep the momentum going and to continue the *new* tradition.

What makes the difference in this story isn't the principal or the staff; instead, it's the parents. The principal can certainly support the After Prom, but she doesn't have the ability to change the culture by herself. Instead, it takes a committed group of parents working with her to make the change.

This sort of situation isn't an isolated occurrence. The truth is, parents have the ability to add tremendous value to a school and a district. Whether it's volunteering in a child's third-grade class, running for School Committee, raising a concern with the principal, or organizing an improved After Prom, there are lots of opportunities for parents to add quality in their children's schools while also serving as a quality control.

This section will tell you how to do that. Chapter 12 looks at ways in which parents can add value within the system, volunteering their time and talents to improve the quality of education in a school. Chapter 13 looks at the other side of the coin: what to do when you are concerned about a school or district practice that you believe should change.

Chapter 12

You Want to Help Out—How Can You Add Value *within* the System?

This chapter focuses on how parents can add value *within* the existing system. You're not trying to change anything; you just want to volunteer your time, expertise, and/or financial resources to make the existing things better.

The chapter begins with a quick survey of what it means to add value, with examples of how that might look. There are plenty of ways you can get involved in your child's school, and understanding the nature of those opportunities is your first step.

Next, the chapter will try to help you identify the types of opportunities that would be of greatest interest and value to *you*, and the logistics of actually getting yourself involved. Finally, there is some advice on how to make the most of your contributions, with a bonus section on the ingredients of successful parent-run support organizations.

EXAMPLES OF WHAT ADDING VALUE LOOKS LIKE

There are lots of ways to get involved in and add value to your child's school, but how you get involved can change from elementary to middle to high. When kids are in elementary school, they typically *love* it when a parent comes to school as a guest reader or a parent volunteer in their class. But once they get to middle school or high school? Forget about it. The last thing they typically want is for a parent to show up and embarrass them in front of their friends.

Here's another real-life scenario: It's the first day of school, and a new sixth-grade parent approaches the principal in the morning. She wants to know if it's okay for her to accompany her son to his locker to help him organize it.

"Of course!" the principal answers. But in his head, he's thinking, "After that boy's friends give him a hard time for this today at lunch, that kid's *never* going to let his parents back in school again."

But not to worry! That same mom could join the Parent-Teacher Organization (PTO), raise money for the Art Club, or help redesign the school's website, and her son wouldn't bat an eye (or probably even be aware that she was doing it).

So, there are lots of ways to get involved, but those options fall into two big categories: direct involvement for immediate value versus more indirect involvement to build longer-term capacity. For the rest of this section, there are some descriptions and examples of these two categories. The next section will help you think about what types of involvement might make the most sense for you.

Direct Involvement to Add Immediate value

These are activities in which you give time, energy, or resources to accomplish an immediate need. Schools thrive on this sort of parent involvement because it adds just-in-time value.

At the elementary level, it's common for parents to volunteer in classrooms. This can mean direct work with students—helping to run a literacy center, being a guest reader in class—or it can mean indirect support, such as helping with photocopying or setting up classroom materials. This sort of support is typically *highly* appreciated. It saves teachers' time, and it can allow them to give more attention to students. It's also possible to volunteer in a middle or high school classroom, but this usually means being a guest speaker on a specific topic, as opposed to just generally helping out.

Chaperoning field trips can happen at any level, although that tends to occur more frequently in elementary schools. But big field trips with overnight stays are fairly common at the middle and high school levels and benefit from parent chaperoning.

Outside of the classroom, there are many opportunities to donate time and energy, especially around extracurricular activities, performances, or special events. This could mean helping set up a science fair, cooking food for a faculty appreciation lunch, doing makeup for a school play, or selling baked goods at a soccer game.

This is an area where parent participation is critical; in many situations, some of these events simply couldn't happen without parent support. For example, imagine a high school where there's a big celebratory breakfast for all the seniors on their last day of school. That's close to an impossible event for the school to run—at that time of year, there are simply too many other things going on. Instead, events like that almost always rely on parents in order to happen.

In addition to time and energy, parents can also donate money. While school and district budgets cover the costs of the basic personnel and materials needed for schooling to happen, there are a host of discretionary activities and resources that are not funded through the operating budget. New uniforms for the field hockey team, travel funds for the science club, or money for a classroom book nook: these sorts of purchases might not happen if parents weren't willing to donate additional money.

Indirect Involvement to Build Capacity

This sort of involvement provides less immediate gratification for the volunteer parent. It's focused less on meeting an immediate need, and more on helping a classroom, school, or district over a lengthier time span.

For example, if you offer to sell baked goods at the middle school football game to raise money for new helmets, you're helping address a short-term need: get those players their new gear! But, if you serve as an officer on the Athletics Boosters, you're helping build capacity: you are making a long-term commitment that goes beyond one specific fundraising goal.

Back at the start of this section, there was the story of the After Prom and a group of parents who helped to resuscitate a fading tradition. Within that event there would have been lots of parents who were *directly* involved: donating gift cards for a student raffle, buying food for the event, or chaperoning the night of the party. The event couldn't be nearly as successful without those parents' direct support.

But an event like that couldn't happen unless a core group of parents has been meeting for months to plan out all the details. That group's work, vision, and commitment is the engine that makes events like that possible.

Schools love, appreciate, and benefit from direct, just-in-time volunteer efforts. But the long-term, capacity-building efforts are what tend to make the big differences over time.

Some of these efforts are focused on a specific goal. For example, parents can serve on a team tasked with picking a new principal, a committee recommending a new math program, or a task force studying a new building project. The After Prom example was a goal-specific activity: plan and implement a specific party on a specific day.

Other efforts are focused on long-term advocacy or improvement. These activities typically require a longer time commitment and are generally open-ended. Being an officer on the Athletic Boosters is an example, or a member of the PTO. Some schools and districts have parent groups that raise money for teacher grants: the teachers can propose projects or materials that are not covered in the regular budget, and the parent group picks which projects to fund.

Parents can also get involved in groups that advise on or set policy, either at the school or district level. The most consequential of these is the School Committee or School Board, which typically creates the policies for the district, decides the district budget, and oversees the superintendent. In some instances, parents may even be able to participate in state-level groups, working with educators and state officials to review or propose state-level practices or policies

HOW TO FIND OPPORTUNITIES TO ADD VALUE

If you want to get involved and add value in your child's school or school system, there are two important questions: What do you want to do, and how do you find a way to do it?

The first question—what you want to do—will likely depend on your motivations, your skill set, and the amount of time you have available. The second question—how to go about actually getting involved—will depend on the nature of what you want to do. The steps for volunteering in the school's library will be different than the steps for becoming the new president of the Athletic Boosters. The rest of this section walks you through the nuts and bolts of answering these two questions.

Figuring Out What You Should Do

As a general rule, parents tend to be most willing to get involved in ways that directly connect to their children's activities and interests; for example, volunteering in their child's classroom or donating money to their child's band program. This doesn't have to be the case—some parents and guardians just like supporting the schools, and they're happy to give their time, energy, or resources to activities not connected to their kids. But that tends to be the exception rather than the rule.

If you already have a sense of what you would like to do, then great! Go ahead and move to the next section. If, however, you're not quite sure what you'd like to do, there's a worksheet in the appendix that can help you. The worksheet will walk you through how the answers to the following three questions can help you pinpoint opportunities that might be a good fit:

- *Why* do you want to be involved?
- What *skill set* do you have to offer?
- How much *time and energy* are you willing to commit?

Figuring Out What's Available and Who to Contact

So, you've thought about how you might want to add value, and you're ready to get involved. What now?

Your next steps will depend on the type of involvement in which you're interested: there's a different path to volunteering in your child's second-grade classroom than there is to becoming an officer of the PTO.

Volunteering in the Classroom or School, Chaperoning, or Helping Class Activities

If you're interested in helping directly with students or class activities, the classroom teacher is your best contact. Especially at the elementary level, it's common for teachers to send home regular newsletters or e-mails with information about the class; definitely make sure you are signed up to receive those, as they may have proactive information for you about how to get involved.

Schools also often send out regular information to parents, typically via e-mail, and that can include updates about volunteer opportunities. A school secretary should be able to check and make sure you are on that distribution list. And finally, the teacher's website or the school's website may have information about volunteer opportunities.

If you are not receiving proactive communication from the teacher, or you can't find information on the class or school website, go ahead and send the teacher an e-mail. Be specific about the ways in which you are interested in volunteering and the time you have available. Just know that what you have in mind, and what will actually be most helpful for her, might not always be exactly the same thing.

The same rules that apply for a teacher's classroom also apply for other spaces or activities in the building. For example, if you are interested in helping out in the library, contact the school's librarian (whose name and contact information should be on the school website, or available if you call the school's main office). Whatever activity interests you, figure out who's in charge and reach out directly to that person.

One last point to keep in mind is that, if your volunteer efforts will bring you into regular contact with students, you'll likely need to have a criminal background check performed. Your school or district should have forms available to do this, and it will require you providing a copy of your driver's license. In some cases, you may even need to have a fingerprint check done. So, don't be surprised if there is some lag time between you expressing your interest in volunteering and actually being able to get started.

Getting Involved in School Events or Parent-Run Committees

If you are interested in helping out with a school event or getting involved with a parent-run committee (such as the PTO), then school newsletters, e-mails, and the school website are good sources of information. Volunteer solicitations will likely be a part of school-parent communication, so make sure you are on the parent distribution list. And many school websites have pages for different groups and organizations, replete with information about how to get involved.

If you aren't able to find specific directions for how to volunteer, reach out to the person in charge. For a school event, such as a play or concert, this will likely be a teacher. For a parent organization, such as the Athletic Boosters or Friends of Music, it will be the president of the group. Once you find their e-mail or phone number, contact them and let them know how you would like to be involved, and how much time you are able to commit.

And, if you aren't able to figure out who the right contact person is, go ahead and reach out to an administrator (the principal or assistant principal)—they should be able to connect you with the right person.

Becoming a Member of a Formalized School Group or Committee

Most of the examples so far are "helping out" activities: helping a teacher or a group with existing activities or plans. And there's no question these are super important ways to add value. But there are also opportunities to get involved in formalized groups that make some pretty consequential decisions.

These sorts of groups—a school building committee, a principal advisory group, or even the School Board—typically have rules or processes for membership. Even being a part of the PTO can have guidelines, especially if you want to become an officer.

Websites are still a good place to start when looking for information about participation, and opportunities for involvement may be included in school newsletters or e-mails. For example, when there's an opening for a new middle school principal, the superintendent may send out an e-mail to all the school's parents inviting volunteers to be on the search team. Other groups have clearly defined rules for participation, such as School Boards or Committees. In most school districts, these will be based on elections and there are formal requirements for throwing your hat into the ring. If that's the case, check out the district's website or the local municipality's website for the process. In some districts, School Board members are appointed by a mayor or other municipal executive, and your ability to participate depends more on political relationships.

Not all opportunities for participation, however, are clearly advertised. Sometimes you have to be "in the know" to find out about them. There are times when principals will take steps to recruit specific parents because the principal knows and respects them, and the principal isn't about to open things up to just anyone. If you are interested in being considered for these sorts of opportunities, you need to let the principal know proactively.

Start by sending the principal an e-mail and asking for a (brief) meeting (this could be a phone call or face-to-face). Explain that you are interested in being involved in the school, and you are looking for ways to do so. When you meet, explain your background, interests, and available time, and make it clear that you would like to be considered if there are opportunities for parent participation on school-level committees. The principal may not have anything available for you at the moment, but this puts your name in the back of her mind and sets you up for future opportunities.

One big piece of advice if you do decide to do this: make it clear that you will not be a difficult parent representative. If the principal leaves the meeting thinking, "Man, that parent would be a headache to manage," then chances are you just ensured that you will *never* make it onto a group. You want the principal to know that you're open-minded, committed to supporting the school, and interested in knowing how you can help. It's okay to be passionate about a specific topic, but you want to show that you will be respectful and work *with* the principal, not against her.

HOW TO MAKE YOUR CONTRIBUTION TRULY VALUABLE

So, you've figured out what you want to do and you've successfully managed the logistics to start doing it. Now, how do you make sure your contribution ends up being truly valuable?

Here are four recommendations to maximize the value of your work. After these four recommendations, there's one final section that is particular to parent-run organizations, such as the PTO or the After Prom planning committee. There are some very specific qualities that make these sorts of organizations successful.

The Four Rules to Making Your Contribution Valuable

To maximize both your contribution to the school and your satisfaction with your efforts, you need to be ready to execute, work within the existing framework, do something that feels meaningful to you, and build relationships with the right people.

Be Ready to Execute

If you've never seen the television show *Shark Tank*, it's highly recommended. In the show, a panel of super-successful business-men and -women hear pitches from budding entrepreneurs. And during one of the episodes, there was a comment that has a lot of relevance for parent volunteers.

As the *Sharks* were debating a business proposal, one of them asked a question: Which is more important, the idea or the execution? In other words, is it better to have a really good business idea or to do a really good job of executing whatever idea you have? The *Sharks* were unanimous in their opinion: execution is more important than the idea. Better to have a mediocre business idea that is executed well, than a great idea that is executed poorly.

The same thing is true when it comes to parent volunteers. There are parents who go to the principal with innovative ideas, but then want to leave it to someone else to do all the heavy lifting. Most principals will find those situations to be completely unhelpful, sometimes even counterproductive. The parents think that all of the value is in their great idea, but just like the *Sharks* know, it's not about the idea, it's about the execution.

So, if you get involved in your child's school—whether it's helping out in the classroom, joining an organization, or helping to raise money for a specific cause—be ready to execute. That doesn't mean that ideas don't matter. A clever or compelling idea *can* be really important. But the greater value comes in rolling up your sleeves and getting the work done.

Work within the Existing Framework

One piece of earlier advice was to not be a "difficult" parent volunteer. If you come in and immediately start telling people what needs to change, chances are you will quickly alienate everyone around you. And this will dramatically decrease your ability to add value.

There may come a time when you *do* have the opportunity to propose and help implement a change. But that only happens after you have proven yourself, built relationships with others, and accrued some social and political capital.

Some parents are super volunteers: they seem to be involved in everything. And when those people have suggestions on how to do something, administrators listen. The reason they listen is because they respect those super volunteers: administrators appreciate their work, and they knew that the volunteers wouldn't propose anything that they're not willing to put time in to implement.

So, you may think the classroom teacher in whose class you are volunteering should run her literacy centers differently. You may think the director of the Fall Play, whose costumes you have volunteered to mend, should pick productions with more speaking roles. Or you may think the middle school principal, whose Parent Advisory Council you just joined, should let all the eighth graders have recess each day after lunch.

My advice? Keep those recommendations to yourself, at least initially. Put your time in, show your value, become the super-helpful parent that everyone appreciates, and work within the existing framework. Then people *will* start listening to you when you share your suggestions. And, if you care so much about making a change that you simply can't be patient, skip to the next chapter.

Do Something that Feels Meaningful to You

This one may seem obvious, but in order to feel good about the contribution you are making, it's important to do something that is meaningful to you. Every time you leave the classroom in which you just volunteered, finish the meeting of the PTO you joined, or hand out the programs at the band concert you helped support, you should have a rosy glow. You should believe you are making a positive contribution and it should make you feel good.

If it doesn't—if you dread managing those rambunctious first graders, or attending all those endless meetings, or getting papercuts after folding your thousandth program—then you should find something else. You won't be happy, and your unhappiness will limit your ability to add value. Instead, find something that *will* give you that rosy glow.

Build Relationships with the Right People

They say that the three most important things in real estate are location, location, and location. Well, the three most important things in schools may very well be relationships, relationships, and relationships.

All types of relationships are important: between teacher and student, teacher and parent, student and student, teacher and teacher, and so on. And what's true everywhere else is also true for parent volunteers. If you can build good relationships with the right people—the teacher in whose class you volunteer, the other parents on the committee to which you belong—you can add better value.

There are many reasons why this is important. Good relationships lead to good and trusting communication. They give you more influence and opportunity to expand your volunteer impact (if that's something you're interested in doing). If part of your goal is to build social and political capital—to get on committees, to be in the know, to give people that extra positive incentive when they make decisions about your child—then relationships are crucially important. They don't mean you can get whatever you want, but they give you an added advantage in advocating for your child.

So, who are the right people? In the classroom, it's the teacher. In the school, front office secretaries can wield immeasurable power within a building. In high schools (and maybe middle schools), department heads/chairs are influential people. Coaches, choral directors, National Honor Society advisors—anyone who's in charge of the organization for which you are volunteering. Principals and superintendents are obviously people of influence, but so are athletic directors, and in some cases, other administrators in central office. On parent organizations, the members of the board are influential people (usually).

Once you figure out who the influential people are, make sure you get to know them. This doesn't mean flattery or adding them to your birthday card list, but make sure you spend time talking with them, asking them about how you can help, and proving that you add value. Even if you want nothing more than to help chaperone a field trip every now and then, a little face-time with the classroom teacher and a relationship that allows for good, clear communication between the two of you is going to help you be a better chaperone.

The Secret to a Successful Parent-Run Organization

This last section goes beyond your individual work as a volunteer and speaks to how volunteer groups can add real value. When it comes to parent organizations, there are a number of key qualities that can mean the difference between a successful group and a group that really flounders. So, here are the essential ingredients to a high-functioning parent-run organization:

1. A core group of committed people—In successful parent-run organizations, no matter how big they may be, there's typically a small, core group of really committed people who do the bulk of the work. They're able to bring in other volunteers to help out when needed, but there's that small group that serves as the engine for the larger organization. Without that core group of people—people who make the time to get stuff done, and who believe strongly in the group's mission—it's unlikely that a group will be successful.
2. Clarity around the group's mission—Speaking of mission, this is another key ingredient: the group needs to know what it's about, and what it's not about. Some groups try to take on too many or inappropriate tasks—a PTO that tries to be a shadow bureaucracy running the school, or Athletic Boosters that want to pick all the teams' coaches. Parent-run groups need to be very clear about what their lane is, they need to be proficient drivers inside that lane, and they need to stay out of other people's lanes.

3. Close coordination with the school—Which leads to ingredient #3. Successful groups really focus on coordinating carefully with the school. If you're part of the Friends of Drama, work closely (and appropriately) with the drama director. If you're in the PTO, keep constant lines of communication open with the principal. This means that group leaders need to meet regularly with their school contacts and ask for direction and guidance (two great questions to ask regularly: "Are we providing you with the right kind of support? How could we better support you?"). Some organizations that are ostensibly supposed to be supportive can become more of a headache than a help. When groups don't take the time to get feedback about whether or not their work is helpful, their efforts can end up having minimal impact.
4. Attention to details in execution—It was said earlier that the execution is more important than the idea, and this is doubly true for parent groups. Whatever the group is doing—from raising money for the band program to planning the After Prom—it's crucially important to plan and execute the details. Make sure everyone knows their assignments, talk through a clear timeline, take good notes, and revisit everyone's progress regularly.
5. Good marketing—The success of a parent-run organization rests in large part on its ability to attract members and to convince the school community (teachers, administrators, other parents) that it is doing valuable work. And that requires good marketing. Whether it's a weekly column in the school newsletter, flyers in the staff room, or a supportive e-mail from the principal, parent-run groups need to get out news of their good work. So, make sure your group is constantly thinking about creative and effective ways to market itself.
6. A succession plan—Attracting new members is important for parent-run groups, but arguably even more important is having an effective succession plan. There are plenty of parent groups that do good work for a couple years, and then fade once their core group of leaders leave (typically because their kids age out of the school). If you want your group to continue adding value over the long term, you need to figure out how to pass the baton from one group of leaders to the next. Some groups will have incoming leaders shadow the outgoing ones for a year. Or they build layers of leadership so that people can try their hand for a couple years before moving onto an executive board. But no matter how they do it, effective groups think carefully about how succession will work among their leadership team.
7. Representation from a broad group of parents—One danger within parent-run groups is that they become too homogenous. It's easy for it to happen: existing members recruit among their friends and social circles for new members, and the group gradually comes to represent a

small "clique" of parents. But this can diminish the effectiveness of the group and its ability to have a broad, positive impact. Now, if you're the Friends of Music you're probably not going to try to recruit parents whose children aren't in the music program. But within the music program, make sure you have broad representation. It can make groups more challenging to manage—the broader the diversity of perspectives and ideas, the harder it can sometimes be to reach consensus and make decisions—but that diversity will ultimately make your group stronger and more effective.
8. Relationships with the right people in the community—It can't be said enough: relationships matter. Within any community, there are movers and shakers who can get things done, or prevent things from getting done. Whether it's the town planning board, a finance committee, or a group of religious leaders, those are movers and shakers that you want on your side. Reach out to them, invite them to a meeting, or even ask them to serve on your group. Their support can enhance and facilitate your group's ability to do good work.

Chapter 13

You Want to Help the System Get Better—How Can Parents be a School's Quality Control?

This chapter assumes that you see something in your child's school or district that frustrates or concerns you, and you want to do something about it. Your frustration might have started with an isolated situation, but your concern now extends beyond that. What do you do?

This chapter will help. It will walk you through a set of strategies to understand and take action about your frustration or concern.

But first, a cautionary tale.

There are times when a school administrator will encounter parents who are unhappy with the way a rule or policy has affected their child, and so they set out to get it changed. In some instances this can be really productive: a parent identifies legitimate flaws, they share their concerns in a respectful and collaborative manner, and their advocacy helps the school improve the way they're doing things.

But then there are other times when it doesn't play out so well.

Here's a real-life story: A parent gets frustrated that his child hasn't been recognized for a school award. His kid is a great student but has missed the criteria for recognition by a small margin. Now, that sort of thing happens all the time. Especially in middle and high schools, where specific grade-point averages (GPAs) or test scores are required for an award, some kids are going to fall just below the bar for recognition.

In most situations, kids and parents accept the outcome. In fact, for many students, the take-away lesson is that they need to work a little harder the next time around, and maybe that would make the difference in helping them receive a future award.

But not this parent. This parent is convinced that his son deserves an award, and if his son doesn't meet the criteria then the criteria must be wrong. As a result, he ends up lobbying the superintendent and the School

Committee to have the criteria changed, wanting it adjusted so that it will include *his* child.

Well, the kid never ends up getting the award. But there are a lot of hurt feelings in the process, and the parent loses a lot of credibility with the school and the school system. After all his complaints and efforts, the parent isn't able to change anything and probably reduces his ability to advocate successfully for his child in the future.

Principals should never begrudge parents their emotional advocacy on behalf of their kids, and they shouldn't expect parents to agree with every decision or policy. In fact, disagreements can sometimes lead to some positive changes. But when parents have a concern, there are more effective—and less effective—ways to handle it. This chapter will give you the tools to be a school's quality control when there are legitimate areas for improvement. It will also help you to know which hills are worth dying on, which aren't, and which just aren't appropriate for you to climb in the first place.

The chapter begins with strategies on how you can better understand the system with which you're frustrated: knowing why your child's school does things the way they do puts you in a better position to advocate for possible improvements. Next, the chapter will look at lanes—before you decide to storm the superintendent's office demanding changes, it's important to have a sense of which decisions are legitimately within parents' purview to influence. Next, the chapter will walk you through advice on how to find and make allies in an attempt to improve the system. Finally, the chapter will end with the nuclear option: looking for a different school when things just don't seem capable of improving.

SEEK TO UNDERSTAND HOW THE CURRENT SYSTEM WORKS

For a principal, it's pretty common to have a parent reach out frustrated about a rule or decision, sit down and listen to the principal explain its rationale, and then, at the end of the conversation, say "Oh, okay, that makes sense." Most school rules and decisions aren't arbitrary—they have clear reasoning behind them, even if that reasoning may not be immediately clear.

At the same time, principals can also have conversations with parents in which, by the end of the conversation, the principal is saying to *himself*, "That doesn't make any sense, why do we do it that way?"

Your first step in addressing a concern is developing an understanding of the existing system that created the concern. Until you do that—let's be honest—you're just a random parent with a random opinion. And savvy principals know that there are *lots* of parents with *lots* of opinions, and they can't respond to all of them.

To get some traction, you need to know what you're talking about. Maybe you think the girls' soccer coach is totally biased in the way she picks players for the team; maybe you think the bus routes have too many kids crossing dangerous streets; and maybe you think the school stresses students out with its ridiculously high homework expectations. But unless you're seen as someone who understands the system—in other words, a parent with an *informed* opinion—chances are you won't get anywhere.

So, if you have a concern and think something should change, use these framing questions to guide you in first understanding the current state of affairs.

What Is the Current System, and Why Is It that Way?

You want to begin by figuring out how the current system works. A lot of information about schools is available online, either through school or district websites, so that's a good place to start. But the true nuts-and-bolts information probably isn't available unless you ask someone for it directly.

In order to get that insider information, you need to identify the right people and ask them for it. When you do this, please be super polite. It's not your job as a parent to evaluate a school's practices—that's the job of administrators and the School Board—so educators can quickly bristle at the thought of some random parent asking aggressive questions. But you absolutely have a right to understand how a school operates. Frame your questions in polite terms and you are much less likely to get stonewalled. A simple way to frame it is: "I have a concern about X, but first I'm interested in understanding the system from your perspective. Would it be possible for me to send you some questions for you to answer?"

If at all possible, get information in writing. It's okay to talk to someone on the phone or face-to-face, but then you need to take really careful notes and check with the educator afterward to make sure those notes are accurate. If you do speak with someone, send them an e-mail after the conversation summarizing the information and ask them if your recollections are correct.

In terms of who to speak with, you want to talk to the person in charge of the system. If you're unhappy with the way kids are picked for the soccer team, start with the coach or the athletic director. If you see problems with the way the school's International Fair is run, find out who's in charge and start with them. If you're worried about allergens in the cafeteria during lunch, talk to the cafeteria manager. You can always contact an administrator—typically a principal or, if it's a district concern, the superintendent—but don't be surprised if they quickly forward you to someone more directly connected to the situation.

When you speak with them, ask questions that will help you better understand the system. Try to put aside any preconceived notions you might have and go in with an open mind. In addition, go to learn, not to challenge (although that may come later).

For example, let's say you think the bus stops create dangerous conditions because kids have to walk long distances to be picked up. The transportation director tells you that the number one priority in building the bus routes is minimizing ride time, so they like to limit the number of total stops. Your next question shouldn't be, "So, you don't care about student safety?!?" A better question would be, "How do you balance minimizing ride time with maintaining student safety?" That question will help you better understand the trade-offs that are being made in the system and put you in a more informed position if you ultimately want to lobby for more stops.

When you ask good questions, it can expose problem areas to decision-makers. It's embarrassing to admit, but principals can at times be clueless about the fine details of how something runs in their building. But, once parents bring specific problems to the principal's attention, it puts pressure on them to do something about it.

One final note: Don't be surprised if you find that "adult convenience" is a driving factor in a system's rationale. Educators work hard, and it's not uncommon for schools to create rules that make educators' difficult job a little bit easier. So, don't be shocked if an underlying rationale for a specific system is that it's most convenient for the adults working in the system.

What Are the Rules, and Who Makes Them?

In addition to understanding how the current system works, you also want to understand the official rules (and where there might be discrepancies between the rules and actual practices).

A good place to start is the district's policies (typically developed by the School Board/Committee) and/or the school's student handbooks. These documents should all be available online; if they're not, ask the school's or district's front office for a copy of them. Two other important documents are the Program of Studies (which lists all of a middle or high school's courses, along with information about school policies) and the faculty handbook. You may not be able to get a copy of the faculty handbook—they are often internal documents and may not be readily made available to parents—but it doesn't hurt to ask. Here's one quick example of how a faculty handbook can be helpful.

A complaint that principals sometimes get from middle and high school parents is around teachers keeping up with grading. Inevitably in any middle or high school, there are going to be some teachers who don't give many assessments over a quarter or term, and/or who are late in giving back graded work to students. At the same time, it's very common for schools to have specific expectations for teachers about assessment quantity and turnaround, and those expectations are commonly found in the faculty handbook. If the English department is notorious for turning back papers late, and you can point to a rule in the faculty handbook that says they should be returned within one week, then it's now up to the principal to start enforcing the rule more consistently.

Which leads to the next important question: Who makes the rules? And there are really two layers to that question: Who is making the rules in practice and who is actually empowered to make the rules? The English teachers may have created their own practice of turning tests back late, but they're not empowered to arbitrarily make that the expectation. The principal, superintendent, and/or School Board members are the ones who are actually empowered to set expectations for teachers.

So, you need to figure out who the governing authority is. For a school-level rule or policy, it's likely the principal, whereas it will be the superintendent and/or School Committee for district-level policies. Athletic rules are probably overseen by an athletic director, food guidelines by a nutrition or food services director, bus routes by a transportation director, and so on. But if in doubt, ask the principal a simple question: "Who's in charge of this rule?" Because the person who's in charge of the rule is very often the one who can change it.

KNOW WHAT IS—AND ISN'T—YOUR LANE

There's an important lesson about lanes that one can learn driving on the highway in Germany.

In the United States, people tend to drive all over the place. They pass on the left, they pass on the right—and sometimes they just pick a lane and stay there, not caring how many people they're holding up.

But not in Germany. There, you drive in the right-hand lane and you only move to the left if you need to pass. And you better not just cruise in the left-hand lane—if you do, pretty soon you'll have a BMW or a Mercedes flying up behind you, barreling along at 200 kilometers an hour and honking at you to get the heck out of their way!

On the Autobahn in Germany, you need to know your lane and you need to stay in it.

There's a lesson here for parent involvement. While you may be frustrated about something happening at your child's school, some things just aren't in your lane. Unfortunately, there are parents who think everything is their lane.

They feel free to tell teachers how to teach, coaches how to coach, and leaders how to lead, and they quickly develop reputations that mean that, more often than not, they just get ignored.

So, as a parent, it's important to know what is and isn't your lane. But (and there is admittedly a bit of a contradiction here), it's also important to know how to sometimes make something your lane that typically wouldn't be.

Understanding the Lanes

There's a reality about decision-making in schools that parents sometimes have a hard time with: lanes aren't defined so much by expertise, or even by being right, as they are by organizational position. You might have a PhD in chemistry from the most prestigious university in the world, but that doesn't mean you get to tell your child's third-grade teacher how to teach a chemistry unit.

When teachers make decisions about what to teach and how to teach it, they do so in part because they are educational experts. But they also do so because they are the people employed and empowered by the school system to make those decisions. Pedagogical decisions are teachers' lanes, even if you, the parent, might actually know better. The same thing is true for administrators. They are the people employed and empowered by the school system to make decisions about student discipline, about scheduling, about teacher assignments, and a whole host of other stuff.

So, pedagogical decisions—what to teach, how to teach, how to test, how much homework to assign—aren't a parent's lane. Similarly, administrative decisions—discipline, personnel evaluations, student recognitions—aren't a parent's lane. And then a lot of the extracurricular stuff—who makes the team, how to coach the team, who picks the musical, who gets the solo in the concert—also aren't a parent's lane.

You may be unhappy about some of those things. You may wonder how that kid ever got the lead in the Spring Play, why your child's mediocre teacher got the Educational Excellence Award, or why the school uses such a high GPA to determine the honor roll. But those aren't your lane.

What *is* your lane, however, is what happens to *your* kid. If your child never gets a part in the musicals, you can ask why. If your child's teacher seems to be ineffective, you can talk to the principal. If your child didn't make the honor roll, you can ask why the school uses a specific GPA. You can't necessarily change any of those things, but it's absolutely your lane to talk about your child's experience within the context of different pedagogical or administrative practices.

It also turns out that, when you talk about your own's child's experiences, that can end up sparking a move to make some changes. Plus, there *are* actually some ways that you can make those pedagogical or administrative practices your lane, which leads to our next section.

Tricks on Switching Lanes

This section begins with an important distinction: the difference between having a *voice* and having a *say*. Having a voice means getting to have some sort of input into a decision—your voice will be heard and noted. Having a say means getting to participate in actually making a decision—more than just being a voice, you get a vote.

Most of the tricks on switching lanes involve having a voice: you figure out a way to have your opinions, thoughts, or ideas become part of a decision-making process. But there are also times when you can maneuver yourself into having a say. In the lane-switching tricks below, it will be highlighted when there are opportunities for parents to become actual decision-makers.

The six ways for parents to switch out of their normal lanes are to:

- Move up the chain of command
- Become a volunteer
- Join a committee
- Participate in public forums
- Run for elected office
- Campaign and vote for elected representatives.

Move up the Chain of Command

This is pretty straightforward—if you don't get traction with the first person you talk to, talk to their boss. This approach also works with astonishing frequency: a parent gets the ear of a decision-maker, has a private conversation, and the decision-maker incorporates that advice into a decision.

There are a couple important things to remember here. First, don't jump straight to the top. Effective leaders will want you to follow a process before they talk to you, so start with the person where the concern originated. When the principal or athletic director or food services director asks, "Have you already talked to the teacher/basketball coach/cafeteria manager?" you want to be able to say "Yes."

Next, don't be a jerk. You want this decision-maker to listen to you and potentially take some action based on your concern. The best way to do that is to treat them as a potential ally, not as an adversary.

Next, be prepared. Be ready to summarize the concern and make a cogent argument, preferably supported by some evidence and facts. If you think the drama director is playing favorites when picking actors for the play, have some evidence, not just rumors or suppositions. And please never say something like "Everyone knows," "It's common knowledge," or "I've got a lot of other parents who agree with me." If everybody knows, then provide some data. If other parents agree, then have them reach out to the decision-maker as well.

Finally, be specific. What exactly is your concern, and what do you see as the remedy? If the district doesn't do enough to support disadvantaged students, what should the district do? If the high school shouldn't use a weighted GPA to determine honor roll, how should they do it?

Become a Volunteer

One of the things about being a volunteer is that it puts you on the inside. You can see first-hand how the system works, you get access to decision-makers, and you build political capital. It's just a fact that, when the president of the PTO expresses an opinion, the principal's much more likely to pay attention than when some random parent fires off an angry e-mail.

So, don't be a random parent. Instead, be someone who knows the school and whom the school knows. This can certainly give you a voice. If you're a volunteer coach, your opinions will matter in team decisions. If you're a member of the Friends of Music support group, you get regular access to the band director.

It can also give you a say. Some parent volunteers and volunteer organizations can have a pretty big impact on school practices. PTO presidents get asked to serve on hiring committees, and PTOs can make decisions about what playground equipment to buy or how the International Festival is going to run. You don't suddenly become a quasi-administrator, but you can certainly maneuver yourself into some decision-making lanes.

Join, or Create, a Committee

This is a good one. Parents can serve on committees that pick teachers, principals, and superintendents. There are committees that pick math programs, recommend building projects, and advise on food allergy policies. School and district administrators regularly tout how they believe in "involving all stakeholders," and they can catch heat if they don't at least give the appearance of having solicited parent feedback on big decisions. You want to be one of those parents.

So, if you have a concern and it doesn't feel like it's being addressed, find a committee that connects to it. There won't be a committee for everything, so this isn't always the answer. But you might be surprised at how many committees are out there.

The easiest way to find a committee is to ask. You can always ask the person who oversees a specific area, but principals aren't a bad place to start. And if it turns out there isn't a committee focused on your concern, propose that one be created (this can be a favorite stall tactic for a frazzled administrator—form a new committee and put all those pesky parents on it—but it actually can lead to some real changes!).

Once you're on a committee, be a good member. That means you need to listen to others—including the teachers and administrators, who actually know a thing or two about schools—and be a respectful member. That doesn't mean you shouldn't make your points and be insistent about what you think is right, but remember that you're one member of a larger group.

In addition, make sure your group has a clearly defined purpose and set of outcomes. Too many committees turn into chances for people to hear themselves talk with no real action or decisions. Also, be clear on whether your committee has a voice or a say. Sometimes parents join a committee that they thought was empowered to make a decision, only to learn at the end of the process that they were simply providing "advice" to an administrator, who was likely to ignore the committee's opinions and just make her own decision.

Don't get me wrong, advisory committees—as opposed to decision-making committees—are super important, and there are many situations in which "advice" is the most appropriate role for a committee. Just make sure it's clear which type your committee is, and how seriously your group's work will be taken.

Participate in Public Forums

It's astonishing how often a small group of vocal parents speaking in a School Board meeting can move the dial on an issue.

School Board/Committee meetings will typically have a time slated for public comment when parents have the opportunity to say whatever they want. In addition, budget meetings frequently have opportunities for public comment, and it's not uncommon for School Boards or other elected officials to schedule forums specifically to allow parents and the community to comment on a topic or decision.

This means that outside of a few no-no topics—for example, complaining about an individual teacher by name, or talking about a specific student disciplinary situation—public forums let a parent make *anything* their lane, if only for a few minutes.

There are, however, more and less effective ways to do this. First of all, there is power in numbers. It's okay to be a lone voice on a topic, but your concerns are far more likely to be given credence if they are perceived as being broadly shared. If you can, get a group of people to show up and all focus on the same topic.

In addition, be careful about crying wolf too often. If you're known as someone who shows up at every forum, always with a new gripe, decision-makers will start to ignore you. So, if you're *that person*, the one who comes to every School Board meeting and feels compelled to complain about every little detail, then you should probably think about the next piece of advice: running for elected office.

Run for Elected Office

This is the ultimate way to make things your lane: get elected as a School Board/Committee member. In that role, you now have the opportunity to set policy for the district, be involved in the development and approval of budgets, and supervise the superintendent.

Despite the opportunities that come with being an elected official, however, even School Board members, mayors, finance committee members, selectmen, city councilors, and so on have defined lanes. For example, being a School Board member doesn't mean that you can now get that bad middle school teacher fired (the one you kept complaining about to the principal). And driving outside your lane can have real consequences. In a real-life story, a School Board member used his power behind-the-scenes to get his son transferred to a different school (despite rules prohibiting it), and then to get a special bus route set up to get his son to and from the new school. Needless to say, when this information hit the local newspapers that School Board member suffered the consequences in the next election.

And, what was true for Spiderman is also true for elected officials: with great power comes great responsibility. It's one thing to complain that the rules kept your child from getting an award (going back to the story that started this chapter), but it's a completely different thing to now change the awards' rules in a way that affects *all* children. As an elected official, you go from being responsible for just your child to being responsible for every parent's child.

Campaign and Vote for Elected Representatives

Maybe running for elected office yourself is more than you want to bite off, but getting involved in local campaigns—and simply taking the time to go vote—are also ways to have an impact.

If you think your child's school system is too punitive in its approach to discipline, campaign for a School Board candidate who says she will look at the discipline policies. If you're worried about the lack of support your child's school gives to non-native English speakers, find out which School Board candidates see that as a priority and vote for them.

If your child is being disciplined, or your child needs more language support, you can certainly express preferences and advocate on your child's behalf. But as a parent, it's not your lane to tell schools how to handle those topics. By campaigning and/or voting for elected representatives, however, you pick the people who *can* make that their lane and do something about it.

FIND AND MAKE ALLIES

This chapter has talked about a number of steps you can take to try to address a concern, but a key component of being able to do so effectively is having allies. Whether it's a group of like-minded parents or influential staff members who share the same concern, you stand a much better chance of success if you're working as part of a cohesive group.

This section will start by looking at how to build parent coalitions, and then switch to talking about building relationships with staff members.

Finding Parent Allies

Another real-life story: A high school coach acts in a pretty unprofessional way at a game, and a number of parents witness the behavior. Several of those parents contact the principal and the athletic director to express their concerns, but the parents each reach out individually. The AD and the principal touch base and create a plan to deal with it, but they're both busy people and this situation isn't at the top of their To Do list.

Then, a number of the parents get in touch with each other, they organize an unofficial meeting of parents, discuss their concerns, and finally send an open letter to the principal and the athletic director signed with all of their names. Suddenly, the situation moves multiple rungs up the priority list, and the principal and AD schedule a meeting right away with the parents.

Now, while this might not be the most advisable way to handle the situation—parents getting together as a group to gripe about a staff member feels a little sketchy—their approach certainly was effective. They found allies, coordinated their message, and put political pressure on the principal and the athletic director to take their concerns seriously. This next part breaks those two steps down and talks briefly about how to accomplish them: first, finding other parents, and then taking coordinated action.

How to Find Other Parents

It's not always that easy to find out if other parents share a concern. It's not like you can call up the principal and ask, "Are there any other parents as unhappy as me with the basketball coach?"

One strategy is to be places where other parents are likely to be. Athletic events, concerts, awards ceremonies, and open houses: they all provide opportunities to meet and network with other parents. Group meetings and public forums are other places where you could meet parents with similar opinions. If you join the Friends of Music and attend their meetings, you will have plenty of opportunities to talk about the details of the school's music program.

Social media is another way to connect. Parents frequently form Facebook pages (or use some other social media site) for classes, teams, or groups, and those sites—and their corresponding message boards—can provide insight into group members' opinions.

It's also not unheard of for a staff member to provide insights. A sympathetic guidance counselor might confirm that other parents are worried about a new school rule, and even suggest other parents to contact.

A key thing with finding other parents, though, is to be careful in the way you raise your concern. Throwing out a group message saying "Who else thinks the world language program is horrible?!?" probably isn't the most strategic approach. Instead, be diplomatic in your questions, raising a topic ("So, what do people think about the world language program?") or putting out a careful hook of concern ("Anyone else who thinks the International Fair could have felt a little more organized?"). If other people share your concern, they'll let you know. And, if all you hear are crickets, then it may be a concern that's particular to you.

How to Coordinate and Implement a Plan

Once you've found allies, the next step is to coordinate and implement a plan. To do this, you have to focus on goals—not emotions—and you need to keep your group in synch on how to move forward.

One of the things that can happen when a group of parents with a similar concern gets together is they amplify each other; there's just an emotional catharsis in *finally* being able to talk about your concerns with someone who gets it. But eventually everyone needs to move past the emotion and figure out an objective. Are you looking for a meeting with the superintendent, a change to policy, or a plan to get your students some extra support?

Figure out what your group sees as a reasonable goal and make sure that goal is in your lane. For example, a meeting with the superintendent is perfectly reasonable and appropriate, but getting a staff member fired is not parents' prerogative.

Once you have a sense of your goal, make sure the members of the group are on the same page as far as your next steps. Are you sending a group letter to an administrator? Are you planning to show up at the next School Board meeting? Are you all going to send coordinated e-mails to the athletic director? If there isn't agreement on next steps, then there is an opportunity for confusion in your actions.

Even worse, there's the possibility that some members will head off the ranch. It's happened before: a group of parents meet, establish a common concern, and then one extra-concerned member tries to amp everything up. Maybe the group decides to just request a meeting, but one member jumps to demanding a change in policy. In any parent group, it's not uncommon for there to be some members who want to co-opt the group to drive their own private goals. Watch out for that, and do your best to keep everyone united in the plan.

BUILDING RELATIONSHIPS WITH INFLUENTIAL STAFF

In addition to finding other parents, a smart approach is to find and build relationships with influential staff members. They can provide you with insider information, and potentially work behind-the-scenes to support you.

As an example, let's say you're frustrated that foreign language instruction doesn't start in your district until middle school, and you're hoping the district will add it at the elementary level. There are lots of possible staff allies who might share your perspective: the chair of the high school world language department, a district curriculum coordinator, middle school world language teachers, and maybe even elementary principals. Those people likely have information about world language enrollment, the benefits of learning another language, knowledge of costs and budget drivers, and so on. They might also know the people in the district who will serve as barriers, and be familiar with historical information about previous attempts to expand foreign languages.

To leverage these possible allies, you need to do three things: find them; meet and learn from them; and figure out how you can work with them.

Finding Staff Allies

Step one is finding possible allies. You will want to look for people connected to the issue or concern who have a natural stake in it. If you're concerned that there aren't enough bus stops, it's possible your child's classroom teacher or the principal might share your concern. If you're worried about the district's food allergy policy, the school nurse might be worried as well. If you don't think there are enough staff to adequately serve the district's population of ELLs, there's probably an ELL coordinator who's also frustrated with staffing levels.

So, reflect on staff who might share your concern, and reach out to them. A short, polite, and straightforward e-mail—"I'm concerned that our ELLs aren't receiving enough attention and service, and I was hoping to get your perspective and advice"—should be enough to get you a meeting.

Meeting and Learning from Staff Allies

The next step is to meet with the staff member. Your goal in this meeting is twofold: to better understand the situation from their perspective, and to start to build a relationship. Before you go into the meeting, write down a list of questions that you're hoping to have answered. Some sample questions might include the following: What do they think about the concern? What data exist about it? Who else might be concerned about this? What has been done about it in the past? What is preventing action from being taken?

In addition to getting information, you're also working to make this person an ally. That means you need to be super polite and respectful, even if you believe they may be part of the problem. Avoid placing blame: keep the conversation focused on what could be done to address the concern, not who caused it. Also ask if there are ways that you could be helping them. Maybe they've been complaining for years about inadequate funding for the ELL program, and they'd love to see some parents request a meeting with the superintendent to create political pressure.

Working with Staff Allies

Once you've found staff allies, maintain the relationship with them. Be sure to send them a follow-up e-mail thanking them for their time, and follow through on any steps that you agreed to. One thing to be very careful about is not treating them as an accomplice—while they may share your concern, they have to be careful about the way they advocate for it. Be respectful of the fact that they have responsibilities as a staff member to work within the system, even though you have the flexibility to work outside the system.

FIGURE OUT WHERE YOU DRAW THE LINE

This chapter ends with the story back from the very beginning of the book. In that story, there was a couple who was dissatisfied with the education that their child was receiving, and who asked for advice on what to do.

You know what they ended up deciding? After puttering along for a couple years, continually frustrated with their child's mediocre experience, they eventually pulled their daughter out and sent her to a different school. They lived in a big district that had some school choice options, and they were able to switch her to another public school. The new school was farther away from home and made their lives more logistically complicated, but they were immediately happier: their daughter had a string of great teachers, her academic achievement improved, and she began to genuinely like school.

The reality is that schools can only do so much. They are tasked with a next-to-impossible job: be all things to all people. If it turns out that your child's school isn't meeting her needs, even after you have used the strategies in this book, then you have a tough decision to make. In that case, make sure you understand your options, and then do what is ultimately in your family's best interests.

Schools Can Only Do So Much

Picture a family with a favorite Italian restaurant. The restaurant has great food, a nice menu, and everything is reasonably priced. But imagine that one night the family shows up at the restaurant, the waiter comes over, and one parent says, "You know what, I'm in a sushi mood. How about a California role and some tuna sashimi?" Then the other parent chimes in, "I don't really like sushi, but I'd love a burger, medium-rare, with a side of curly fries." The daughter places her order—General Gao's chicken with some steamed vegetarian dumplings—and the son figures out what he wants: chicken-pot-pie.

The waiter, of course, would look at this family dumbfounded before making it abundantly clear that none of those choices are available on the menu.

But let's further imagine that the state passes a law that says all restaurants must provide whatever patrons would like. Order sushi in an Italian restaurant? They've got to make it. Somebody wants curly fries? Fire up the deep fryer. And the kids' vegetarian dumplings and chicken-pot-pie? Well, the state says that they get to have it.

Can you imagine the kitchen that the restaurant would need to have? And what would gradually happen to the quality of their Italian food over time? The fact is, it's really hard for a restaurant—or any organization, for that matter—to be all things to all people.

That's the challenge that schools face: they serve a wide variety of kids with lots of different strengths and needs, and schools are supposed to serve *all* of them equally well. When a child shows up who needs a specific set of services, schools don't get to say, "Sorry, that's not on the menu."

In reality, lots of schools do lots of things really well, but very few will do *everything* well. One school might have a fantastic program for students with significant cognitive needs, but really struggle to meet the needs of students with English language needs. Another school might be great at supporting struggling kids, but not do much to challenge high-achievers. Or vice versa.

As a parent, you have to decide if your child's school has the right strengths to meet your child's needs. The hope is that this book will help you advocate effectively for your child if they don't, but advocacy might only get you so far. If that's the case, you can either accept a mediocre educational experience, or you can explore other options.

Understand Your Options

This is one of the real challenges of the public education system: for better or worse, a child's educational options are largely determined by their zip code. Wealthier families might have the financial wherewithal to explore private schools, but most people don't have that flexibility. That doesn't mean, however, that parents have no options when it comes to their child's school. The following categories may or may not apply to you, but they are worth knowing about and exploring.

In-district School Choice

This is what the couple at the start of the book took advantage of. Their school system was large enough that it provided opportunities for parents to send their children to different schools within the overall system. In larger districts, there may be magnet programs that attempt to attract wealthier families to schools in less-advantaged neighborhoods and allow for students in those lower-wealth neighborhoods to have options elsewhere in the district. In-district choice can even exist in smaller districts, especially at the elementary level, where parents may be able to pick their child's school (or request it, at least) from a list of options.

Where in-district choice exists, it's important to understand both how the system works and your choices. There will likely be deadlines and rules governing the system, so make sure you educate yourself on the process. But perhaps even more important is understanding how different schools differentiate themselves.

It's important to visit potential schools and speak with people who know them. This could be parents who already go to the school, it could be teachers, or it could be the principal. Your goal is to have a sense of what a school sees as its strengths and to reflect on whether or not those strengths make sense for your child.

Even when a district does not have a choice program, there might be opportunities to have your child move from one school to another. If you're unhappy with your child's education, don't be afraid to ask administrators about the possibility of your child moving schools. You will likely first hear "No" as your answer, but keep pushing if you truly believe your child is not being well-served where she is and could be better served elsewhere.

Charter Schools

Charter schools are independently run public schools that are typically "chartered" directly by the state rather than by a local district. There aren't a ton of them out there, and they have to follow a lot of the same rules as public schools, but they do have autonomous structures and frequently have significant flexibility in terms of curriculum and focus.

In order to get into a charter school you may need to enter a lottery. Contact the school (or check out their website, or both) to find out how the entrance process works. You may also need to be able to get your child to and from school since charter schools are unlikely to offer busing. But even more important than the logistics of how to get into or get to the school is determining whether or not it would be a good fit for your child.

As advised above, take some time to visit a school and find out what makes it tick. Talk to teachers, parents, and administrators and ask what they see as the school's strengths. If you can, read any evaluations you can find of the school, and see if how they market themselves matches the findings of those evaluations.

Charter schools face the same challenges as any school—trying to hire good teachers, working to support the needs of a wide range of kids, keeping students safe—so it's not like the name "charter" connotes any intrinsic advantage. The research literature generally suggests that there are effective and ineffective charter schools, and they are not substantively superior to traditional public schools. But, they do tend to have more specialized menus.

Whereas a traditional public school serves anyone who happens to live in the neighborhood, a charter school serves a self-selected group of families who have chosen the school for particular reasons. This means that charter schools can design and market themselves to emphasize particular strengths. If your child's public school isn't meeting his unique set of needs, it's possible that there is a charter school out there that might.

Private Schools and Voucher Programs

The proviso about charter schools also applies to private schools: there is nothing that makes a private school inherently better than a public school, and there are good ones and bad ones out there.

With private schools, what you are paying for may be smaller class sizes and a self-selected student body. The kids at a private school are there because their parents specifically chose to send them, which allows a private school to focus on a more specialized menu of services. Some private schools offer a religious component that is important to families, others offer a specialized curriculum, and still others offer a sense of exclusivity with a hefty price tag.

Much as is true with charter schools, do your homework. Learn as much as you can about the school and decide whether or not it will be a good fit for your child. And don't assume that just because it costs an arm and a leg that it will provide a superior education to your local public school.

Two final points about private schools. First, some children may qualify for what is called an "out-of-district placement" from their assigned public school as a result of an identified disability. Students who qualify for special education services whose public school clearly is not able to meet their needs can oftentimes attend a specialized private school at district expense.

Second, in some states, the government offers vouchers for parents to send their children to a private school without having to pay the full tuition. These programs tend to focus on students in less-advantaged areas or students who qualify for special education. They do, however, tend to be few and far between; if your state does offer voucher programs, you should be able to find information about them through your state's website.

Homeschooling and Online Education

Two final options are homeschooling and online education. With homeschooling, a family decides to educate their child at home, following a curriculum that they put together. Rules around homeschooling vary from state to state, but if you're interested in homeschooling your child, expect that you will need to go through some type of approval process.

Online education can occur in a variety of ways. An increasing number of public schools offer students the opportunity to take courses online, there are charter schools that are run completely online, and parents choosing to homeschool their child may rely heavily on an online curriculum, especially for high school-age students.

Both of these options generally require a significant time commitment, and potentially a financial commitment from parents. This means that they may not be realistic for lots of families. One of the big advantages of these options, however, is that they remove geography as a barrier. If you live in a rural community, or in an area where there just aren't choices available besides your local school, homeschooling and online education may be the only viable alternatives.

Even when they are viable, you would be cautioned to think long and hard before choosing to homeschool your child or rely heavily on online education. They can be a great choice for some students, but it's hard to reproduce the dynamic of a live classroom with a professional, trained educator. If you are considering these options, it's strongly recommended that you take time to research them and talk to other parents who have chosen them.

Make a Decision That Is Ultimately in Your Family's Best Interests

Some public educators might not be happy to see the descriptions of alternatives in the preceding section. Teachers and administrators are committed to their schools, and they worry that other options—especially charter schools or private schools—can lead to money shifting away from traditional public schools. At the end of the day, educators are interested in advocating for and protecting their institutions as places for all children.

For you the parent, however, it's about figuring out what is best for *your* child. The hope is that this book will help you get the best for your child in their public school experience, but you need to ultimately make decisions that are in your family's best interests. If you're not happy, you've done what you can to try to make things better, but it's still just not working, then you need to look at your options and make the best decision for your child.

Section 1 Appendix

SEEING THE QUALITIES OF EFFECTIVE TEACHERS IN ACTION

As a reminder, here are the traits that define excellence in teaching:

1. Good teachers care.
2. Good teachers are organized.
3. Good teachers set big goals for their kids and for themselves.
4. Good teachers provide lots of feedback.
5. Good teachers have deep content knowledge.
6. Good teachers are with-it.

The following two vignettes provide concrete examples of what these traits look like in practice. They come from actual classroom observations. A classroom observation is a formal evaluation of a teacher while he or she teaches in the classroom—essentially, it means sitting in on a classroom lesson and taking notes on what happens.

These examples are taken from two particularly memorable lessons that were observed by teachers in different schools: Sue and John. Sue was a middle school math teacher and a genuinely nice person. Unfortunately, Sue was a truly lousy teacher. In contrast, John was a kindergarten teacher and a real rock star in the classroom. As you read the stories of each of their lessons, think about how the "good teacher" traits above are either evident or missing.

The Story of Sue

First is the story of Sue's lesson. Sue had invited her principal to come and observe a sixth-grade math lesson, and it began pretty typically for Sue: students wandered in late, with no clear expectations for what they should be doing as they arrived. Once the class settled down and Sue was ready to start, she made an unusual request: "I want everyone to put their textbooks, notebooks, and pencils away." Sue was introducing a new concept—how to add and subtract fractions—and she had decided that she wanted her students' full attention.

For the next half hour, Sue projected onto the whiteboard at the front of the room a PowerPoint presentation that took students step-by-step through the process of adding and subtracting fractions. She included some mathematical vocabulary and plenty of example problems. Occasionally a student would pick up his notebook and begin to take notes. When Sue noticed, she was immediate with her response: "Put your notebook away, I need you paying attention to me and not getting distracted."

When a student raised her hand with a question, Sue's response was equally direct: "No questions now, I will answer your questions later."

It was clear that Sue was proud of her PowerPoint. It had color illustrations, nifty graphics, eye-catching transitions, and even some entertaining audio clips. It was also clear that at least 80 percent of the students were not paying attention. From the back of the room, students could be seen whispering to each other, surreptitiously working on homework for other classes, or just staring out the window.

Once Sue finished her presentation, she gave the students some example problems to work on themselves, and she began to circulate. Many of the students were compliant, doing their best to solve the problems, but since Sue had forbidden them from taking notes they lacked a real understanding of what they were trying to do. Other students simply ignored their math work and instead chatted about their weekend plans (until Sue got close, at which point they would pull out their math books and attempt to look busy, which usually fooled Sue).

As Sue wandered around, she became increasingly frustrated. "No, that's not how you do it." "Melissa, stop talking and do your work." "Brad, I just explained this, weren't you paying attention?"

As the bell rang and the students shuffled out, Sue gave the principal a big smile. "That went pretty well. The PowerPoint came out great!"

The Story of John

John's lesson was also an invited observation (meaning he had asked his principal to come see this specific lesson, as opposed to the principal dropping by his classroom unannounced). The whole school had been focusing on trying to improve students' writing abilities, and John wanted the principal to come see a writing lesson in his class.

At the beginning of the lesson, John had all of his kindergartners gathered and sitting in a carpeted area, while he sat in a rocking chair next to an easel with white paper. The focus of the lesson was on the importance of spacing between words, a skill that is notoriously difficult for kindergartners. John started by writing a couple simple sentences on the paper, making sure not to include any spacing between words. Students quickly began to giggle and call out, "That's not right!" John paused and looked at his sentence: "It's not? What could possibly be wrong with it?" Students called out in chorus, "There are no spaces between the words!"

After "realizing" his mistake, John then rewrote his sentence, using small plastic spaghetti and meatball stickers to mark the spaces between his words (spaghetti went between words, meatballs went between sentences). Throughout, John asked students questions about what he was writing: "Where should the next space go?" "Do I need some spaghetti or a meatball here?" "Why wouldn't I use just spaghetti for that space?"

After finishing the brief lesson, students were dismissed in small groups back to their seats, where they took out writing folders and began working on their own writing. As he sent them to their seats, John also asked a student to turn on the "quiet light," indicating that students needed to work silently. After quickly circulating to make sure students were on task, John then began calling individual students over to him so that he could check their work. He spent a couple minutes with each child, having them read him their writing and giving them a few comments of praise, and a skill to work on: "I love the way you are using spacing between your words. The next thing I want you to be working on is your punctuation—remembering to put periods at the end of each sentence."

While students worked, they had the opportunity to move around the room. Several students found comfortable places to sit while they wrote. Other students went up to the front of the room to check the classroom's "word wall" for how to spell individual words. Every couple minutes, John would scan the room and check to see that students were working, with a quick reminder to any kindergartener whose wiggles seemed to be appearing.

Finally, for the last couple minutes of the lesson, John brought the class's attention back to him and asked for volunteers to read their work. Hands shot up, and John called on several children to read what they had written that day, with applause from the whole class as each student finished. As the lesson concluded, John called students by table to put their writing folders away in color-designated bins on the side of the room. As the principal crept out the door, John flashed a quick smile and began transitioning into the next lesson.

Spotting the Effective Teacher Qualities

So how did the "good teacher" qualities manifest themselves in Sue's and John's lessons? Were you able to spot any patterns? Following are a few examples of how Sue and John either did or did not exemplify the qualities of an effective teacher.

(1) Good Teachers Care

Sue was a pleasant woman and could be very nice to kids at times. But she frequently became frustrated with her students, and her language and actions left a lot of students wondering whether she really liked them. In contrast, John cared deeply about his students and was energized by his interactions with them every day. He ran a tight ship, and students knew that he had high expectations for them, but his enthusiasm for his students and their learning translated into incredibly high levels of motivation and engagement.

(2) Good Teachers Are Organized

No classroom needs and benefits more from organization than a kindergarten classroom. John had distinct spaces set up in his room for different types of lessons, he had visual cues to help students understand his expectations (the "quiet light" for example), he had identified areas for student work, and he had clear routines for student movement throughout the lesson. Sue's lesson was a bit of a mess. While her fancy PowerPoint took her hours to develop, most of the students ignored it because of the way she structured her lecture. And once the lecture was finished, she had no clear expectations or accountability mechanisms for the work that students would do.

(3) Good Teachers Set Big Goals for Their Kids and for Themselves

In Sue's case, she was more interested in a compliant audience for her fancy PowerPoint than in a class of inquisitive students. John, in contrast, took the time to review the work of his students individually and to challenge them to constantly improve. No matter how much a kid struggled, or how much a kid excelled, he was always pushing them to keep pushing themselves.

(4) Good Teachers Provide Lots of Feedback

In Sue's lesson, the students received essentially no feedback, other than exasperation when they weren't successful. John's classroom was full of feedback, both in whole-group and individual contexts. At the beginning of the lesson, he used an interactive writing activity to coach the students on the correct use of spacing. During the quiet writing time, he provided students with specific feedback about their individual work.

(5) Good Teachers Have Deep Content Knowledge

John understood the writing process and the areas with which kindergartners would struggle. He also knew simple tricks to help them improve their writing, such as the spaghetti and meatballs example. Sue treated math simply as information to be disseminated, and her inability to structure activities that appropriately engaged students contributed to her students' apathy and frustration.

(6) Good Teachers Are With-it

Sue most definitely lacked with-itness. She was clueless about the fact that most of her students were disengaged during the PowerPoint presentation, and students were regularly able to trick her by appearing to be busy when they were really just wasting time. John was always with-it, anticipating when students might begin to get antsy and projecting a constant sense of calm and control.

SPOTTING THE QUALITIES OF EFFECTIVE TEACHERS

The descriptions in table A.1 help to provide additional detail on the six qualities of effective teachers.

Great Teachers

...	Positive Signs	What to Look For?
Care	• The teacher makes an effort to get to know your child. • The teacher works with you as a partner for your child's success. • The teacher cares about your child's academic and social development. • Your child believes that the teacher cares about him. • The teacher is generally respected by students and parents.	• In parent-teacher conferences, in e-mails, or in casual conversations, the teacher is able to describe your child's personality, both as a learner and as a person. • The teacher offers opportunities for your child to stay for extra help before or after school. • When providing feedback about your child, the teacher's descriptions are positive and kind, even when describing negative traits. • The teacher contacts you proactively with information about your child, whether positive or negative (e.g., letting you know that your child's grade is slipping, or that he is having trouble with a classmate). • When you ask your child, "Do you think your teacher cares about you?" your child is able to explain why. • Your child's friends and other parents express positive feedback about the teacher.
Are organized	• The teacher communicates proactively with parents about the class. • The teacher responds quickly to questions. • The teacher can describe in detail the work students are currently doing, and the work they will be doing in the future. • The teacher provides lots of assessment opportunities (quizzes, grades, projects, papers, etc.) and returns graded work quickly.	• A class web page has clear and helpful information, and/or the teacher provides a regular newsletter or parent information e-mail. • E-mails are responded to within forty-eight hours. • At a meet-the-teacher night, the teacher has a clear presentation on class expectations and curricula. • During a parent-teacher conference, the teacher can speak in detail about your child's work and progress. • When you ask your child, "Do you know what you are supposed to be learning about, and how you will be graded?" your child is able to provide a clear answer.

Section 1 Appendix 155

	- You see graded work (or work with feedback) returned quickly and regularly.
- An electronic grade book is kept up-to-date, with grades taking no longer than a week to be posted after an assignment has been handed in.
- The teacher sends out regular information to parents that demonstrates considerable time and effort on the teacher's part.
- When you ask a question or send an e-mail, the teacher's responses reflect depth and detail on the topic.
- You see the teacher's name listed as someone who has other responsibilities in the school.
- In meet-the-teacher presentations, parent-teacher conferences, or teacher-provided class information (e.g., newsletters), the teacher talks explicitly about the importance of effort, using terms such as "growth mindset."
- The teacher has identified times when they are available to provide extra help to students before or after school.
- During a parent-teacher conference, the teacher has a clear sense of what your child's areas of strength and growth are, and can speak to big-picture goals both for the whole class and for your child individually.
- In conversations with the teacher about your child, the teacher emphasizes what they *can* or *could* accomplish, not what they can't do.
Set big goals for their kids and for themselves	- The teacher seems like someone who works hard.
- The teacher has other responsibilities in the school or district, such as running an after-school club or activity.
- The teacher regularly emphasizes effort, persistence, and hard work as keys to success and improvement.
- The teacher provides extra help for students when needed.
- The teacher regularly works to improve him- or herself as an educator.
- You are impressed with the depth of what your child is learning.

(continued)

156 Section 1 Appendix

Great Teachers ...	Positive Signs	What to Look For?
Provide lots of feedback	• The teacher regularly assesses your child's academic progress. • The teacher uses multiple types of assessments and has sophisticated ways of judging the quality of student work. • The teacher has an in-depth understanding of your child's strengths and weaknesses. • Your child has a clear sense of what he needs to work on to improve. • The teacher has structures in the class to allow for individualized feedback. • The teacher emphasizes student growth over the attainment of specific grades.	• You see examples of a wide range of work and assessments, including quizzes, tests, projects, essays, presentations, etc. • Graded work frequently includes rubrics with clear descriptions of what quality looks like. • During a parent-teacher conference, the teacher provides multiple examples of your child's work and connects that work to curricular expectations and your child's progress. • In conversations with the teacher about your child, the teacher can speak in detail about your child's areas of academic strength and weakness. • When you ask your child, "What are you good at in your class, and what do you need to work on?" your child is able to provide clear answers. • When describing the class structure, the teacher mentions activities that allow for individualized feedback (e.g., reading groups, one-on-one conferences, seminars). • In teacher newsletters, on the teacher's webpage, and/or in course syllabi, the teacher explicitly emphasizes the importance of student growth as a class goal.
Have deep content knowledge	• The teacher has a clear understanding of the curriculum and the associated student skills and knowledge necessary to master it. • The teacher uses a variety of instructional activities/approaches to help students succeed. • The teacher has a strong background in pedagogy and curriculum. • The teacher regularly works to augment his expertise. • The teacher is recognized as a curriculum expert.	• Teacher-provided newsletters or web pages highlight the curriculum in detail. • During back-to-school presentations, the teacher is able to describe in-depth critical knowledge and skills that students will learn, and a variety of activities in which students will participate. • During parent-teacher conferences, the teacher can describe in detail the academic knowledge and skills that the class will focus on over the course of the year, and can describe a variety of different instructional approaches and the connection between those approaches and student learning.

- If the teacher provides professional information about himself, there is evidence of curricular expertise (e.g., graduate degrees, advanced certifications) and ongoing attempts to improve his expertise (e.g., participation in workshops or conferences).
- The teacher works as a curriculum expert in the district or in a private capacity (e.g., as a consultant or tutor).
- Teacher-provided newsletters, webpages, and/or syllabi include clear and logical behavioral expectations.
- In conversations with other parents or with your child, you hear about minimal (or no) behavioral issues in the class.
- If there are opportunities to observe the teacher with students, she appears to interact comfortably and confidently with them.
- When you ask your child, "Does your teacher have control of the class?" the answer is a clear "Yes."
- When you ask your child, "Do you respect your teacher?" the answer is also a clear "Yes."

Are with-it
- The teacher has a comprehensive and effective approach to managing student behavior.
- The teacher has a strong presence with students.
- Students respect the teacher and behave appropriately in class.

LIST OF PHRASES TO USE IN DESCRIBING YOUR ELEMENTARY-AGE CHILD

If your child's school asks you for information about your child to help in making teacher assignment decisions, the phrases listed in table A.2 will help.

Your Child's Qualities	Phrases to Communicate those Qualities for a Good Teacher Match
Your child has high achieving skills	"My son benefits from an environment in which he will be challenged and stretched."
Your child has high energy	"My daughter benefits from a structured environment with clear directions and expectations."
Your child can be anxious about school	"My child benefits from a teacher who is especially good at creating a comfortable environment and establishing positive, supportive relationships with students."
Your child can easily become bored	"My son works best when he has opportunities to explore his interests, and is given the flexibility to pursue challenging tasks."
Your child struggles academically	"My daughter benefits from a teacher who will support her academically while still setting high expectations."
Your child is social and can become distracted	"My son benefits from a teacher with high expectations who can help him stay focused and help him realize his potential."
Your child has a history of behavioral challenges	"My daughter has had difficulty following classroom rules at times, and benefits from a teacher who is patient, who has consistent expectations, and who collaborates regularly with parents."
Your child is learning to speak English	"My son is still learning to speak English effectively, and benefits from a teacher with a deep understanding of how to support English learners."
Your child struggles as a reader	"My daughter benefits from a teacher with a strong knowledge of reading pedagogy, who can provide targeted reading interventions while also challenging struggling readers to excel."

SAMPLE LETTER ABOUT CHILD FOR TEACHER SELECTION

Start with a brief introduction that specifies the purpose of the letter. What you really want is for your child to get a great teacher, but that's not what you should say (most schools will likely not allow you to request a specific teacher). Instead, use terms like "fit" or "selecting a classroom" to avoid putting the school in an awkward position.

I wanted to write and provide you with information about my child to help you in selecting his classroom next year. I know how important it is to find a good fit between child and class; I hope this letter is helpful in supporting your process.

Give the school a sense of your child's personality. If you're hoping for a specific teacher and you know a bit about that person's interests—for example, maybe they're the advisor for the after-school Legos Club—highlight places where the teacher's personality and your child's overlap.

> My son is a creative thinker and loves to build. Nothing makes him happier than sitting down with a new Legos set and figuring it out! At the same time, he has less patience for artistic activities, strongly preferring to build than to draw.

The bulk of the letter should focus on your child's academic strengths and weaknesses. This letter shouldn't just be a marketing pitch—you want to accurately capture who your child is as a learner. But you can emphasize areas that you think connect directly to a specific teacher or type of teacher.

> My daughter loves math and has shown a real strength with numbers from a young age. But she is not an avid reader, and has struggled to stay at grade level with her reading skills. She would really benefit from a teacher with a strong grasp of early literacy, and someone who can help her develop a love of reading.

In addition to academic strengths and weaknesses, talk about your child's social-emotional skills. This is especially important if you are trying to avoid a teacher that you believe would be a bad personality fit.

> My son has several friends, but he can struggle to connect with students socially. He tends to be anxious in new situations or when put on the spot in front of others. He does best when he is able to develop a positive and nurturing relationship with adults who really show that they care about him.

In addition to social-emotional information, talk about the type of classroom structure that you think will work best. Is your child able to handle less structure? Does she need very clear expectations? Does she feel stifled by rigidity, or does she crave the comfort of routine?

> My daughter has okay organizational skills, but she really benefits from clear expectations and routines. She is less successful in situations where rules or expectations are ambiguous, or when the class structure changes from day to day.

You talked about your child's personality earlier, and maybe made passing reference to the teacher's personality. Here is where you should really talk about the adult personal qualities that you see as the best fit for your child, skewing the narrative toward a desired teacher and away from an undesired teacher.

> My son has been most successful with teachers who have high energy and a consistently positive attitude. He tends to feed off of adults' enthusiasm, and it is very important to him that he feels a strong connection to his teacher. He responds most effectively to positive reinforcement and praise, and does not do as well with adults who have a "strict" personality or tend to rely largely on punishments to manage student behavior.

Section 2 Appendix

QUESTIONS TO ASK WHEN YOUR CHILD GETS INTO TROUBLE WITH AN ADMINISTRATOR

If your child has gotten into trouble with an administrator at school, consider asking the following questions to give yourself as full a picture as possible of the situation. You don't *have* to ask these questions—and an administrator may pre-emptively address them—but they focus on the kind of information that can help you better understand the situation and how it was handled.

Due Process Questions

- How did the school become aware of the situation?
- Has my child had a chance to explain his perspective on what happened?
- Does my child understand what he did?
- Who interviewed my child about what happened?
- If your child has an IEP or requires ESL support, was a special educator or ESL teacher present when my child was interviewed (schools aren't generally required to do this, but it can be an effective practice in certain circumstances)?
- Did my child make any claims that other students have treated him inappropriately? If so, has that been investigated?
- Where in the Student Handbook does it talk about student behavior and the behavior my child exhibited?
- If your child was searched, how was that search conducted?
- If a police officer was involved, did they speak to your child?

Questions about Evidence

- Have you interviewed other students about what happened? If so, what information did they provide?
- Did any staff members witness what occurred? If so, what information did they provide?
- Is there other evidence besides what you've heard from witnesses?
- Are you still collecting evidence, or is that process finished?
- How confident are you about the evidence you have?

Questions about Consequences and Connection to School Rules

- If you've already made a decision about consequences, what is the decision? Why those consequences specifically?
- How do the consequences my child is receiving compared to the consequences other students have received for similar behavior?
- Does the Student Handbook or other school rules specifically address the consequences associated with what my child did?

Questions about How Your Child Was Treated during the Process

- How did my child react during the process?
- What's your sense of how my child is feeling right now?
- Does my child seem to think he's guilty?
- If your child has already been assigned consequences, how did he react to that?

QUESTIONS TO ASK THE SCHOOL IN SIGNIFICANT DISCIPLINARY SITUATIONS

In the cases of a significant disciplinary situation, such as a long-term suspension, ask the following questions when you meet with the school administration:

- How will this disciplinary situation be reflected in my child's educational record (especially relevant for students in high school who receive a transcript)? Will this information or could this information end up being shared with anyone outside the school? What are the privacy rules around protecting the information from this situation?

- What could happen to my child if she gets into further trouble at school?
- What are the future academic ramifications of this situation? Could this impact my child's ability to access future programs or educational opportunities?
- Could this situation limit my child's ability to participate in extracurricular opportunities now or in the future? Could this lead to my child being removed from existing extracurricular groups?
- How will my child receive and complete work while out of school? Who is responsible for coordinating work while my child is out?
- Will the work my child completes mirror exactly what is happening in school? Are there opportunities for my child's work to be diminished so that she is focusing on the most important content, but not necessarily every assignment?
- How will work be handled that cannot be done outside of school? For example, how will she complete labs in science class, or participate in performances for music class?
- Are there options for my child to be tutored at district expense while suspended?
- Are there opportunities for my child to complete online courses in place of just sending work home from the school?
- When my child returns to school, what is the plan to help get her back on track academically?
- My child is in her senior year of high school—how will this impact college applications or existing college acceptances?
- Is my child ever allowed to be on the school campus during her suspension? Can she attend extracurricular activities at school?

If your child has an IEP or is in an ELL program, here are additional questions to ask:

- How will my child continue to receive special education and/or English as a Second Language services while suspended?
- Does this suspension have implications for the detail of her special education and/or ELL plan?
- Does my child have any special protections as an identified student with a disability and/or limited English proficiency?

If your child is being incarcerated or placed into an alternative school for a period of time, here are additional questions to ask:

- Who is responsible for educating my child during this time? Her current school or the alternative setting (this could include a site where your child is being legally detained)?

- How will the school and the alternative setting communicate?
- If/when my child returns to school, how will the school "count" the work done at the alternative setting? How will credits work (if your child is in high school)?
- If/when my child returns to school, how will she be reintegrated back into classes? Will she have to complete any work that happened while she was out, or will the work done at the alternative setting take the place of work done at the school?

If your child is being threatened with the possibility of expulsion, here are additional questions to ask:

- What do state law and district policies say about my child's educational opportunities as an expelled student? What educational responsibilities do the district and state still have to my child?
- Are there any public alternative school options available for my child?
- Is my child eligible to enroll in a different public school in the district or in an alternative district?
- Is expulsion permanent, or is there an opportunity for my child to return to school at some point in the future?

Section 3 Appendix

PICKING A WAY TO GET INVOLVED IN YOUR CHILD'S SCHOOL

To help you figure out ways to get involved in your school or district, think about the following three questions and use the information in the tables provided:

- Why do you want to be involved?
- What skill set do you have to offer?
- How much time and energy are you willing to commit?

Why Do You Want to be Involved?

The first thing to consider is your motivation. Some parents just want to support their child. Other parents see volunteering as a way to meet people and build new relationships. Still other parents see volunteering as a way to build social and political capital, maybe giving them the opportunity to influence decisions made about their child (e.g., the president of the PTO might hope that his child gets assigned the best teachers).

Whatever your motivation—or motivations—it's important to reflect on them before getting involved. The last thing you want is to give your time and energy, only to figure out that the focus of your volunteering isn't something you particularly enjoy.

Why Do You Want to be Involved? Do You Want to . . .

Spend Time with Your Child?	Get to Work with Children in General?	Connect to an Area of Interest or Expertise?	Meet other Parents?	Influence Decisions?
If so, look at activities directly connected to your child's class, like being a guest reader, a regular volunteer in the classroom, or a chaperone on a field trip.	If so, look at activities that put you in direct contact with students, like being a lunchroom volunteer, a chaperone on a field trip, or a Field Day volunteer.	If so, look at activities that connect to that interest, like helping build sets for the play, running a food drive, or serving on a planning committee to build a new school.	If so, look at helping with larger school activities like an International Festival, or joining a parent-run group like the Athletic Boosters.	If so, look at joining a formal group like a search committee for a new principal, or run for local elected office.

What Skill Set Do You Have to Offer?

After figuring out your motivation, the next thing to consider is what you have to offer. Are you super organized, and you're good at helping other people stay on track? Do you have specific academic or vocational skills that would make you a good guest lecturer or an invaluable addition to an activity or event? If you have a financial background, there's bound to be a fundraising group that would *love* to have you as their new treasurer (a perennially difficult position to fill).

You certainly don't have to volunteer in a way that connects to a specific skill set—you could be an astrophysicist, but you're perfectly happy to sit in the school's front office and stuff envelopes. But, as a general rule, parent volunteers tend to feel most rewarded when they are able to combine a particular area of expertise or skill with a specific need or opportunity at a school.

What Skill Set Do You Have to Offer? Do You Have . . .

A Facility for Working with Children?	A Specific Area of Expertise?	Organizational and/or Leadership Skills?	No Particular Skill Set?
If so, look at opportunities that will put you in direct contact with kids, like volunteering in a classroom, supervising students during recess, or helping lead an after-school club.	If so, look at opportunities to leverage that expertise, like being a guest lecturer in a high school classroom, joining a specialized committee, or supporting connected activities or events.	If so, look at longer-term commitments like being a "room parent," larger activities that require significant organization, or committees with leadership openings.	No worries! Stay away from more specialized opportunities, like being treasurer for the PTO and offer yourself up to help out in any activities that match your motivation and availability.

How Much Time and Energy Are You Willing to Commit?

The last question to consider is how involved you can become. If you have a lot of discretionary time, you may be willing to volunteer on a regular basis, spending lots of time on school activities. Maybe you don't have a ton of time, but you're willing to commit to one evening a month. Or, your available time may be seasonal, allowing you to work on a big project in the Fall, but not for the rest of the year.

Whatever your answer, figure it out *before* you make a commitment. There are plenty of parents who start with good intentions, but don't realize how much time the Athletic Boosters can suck up, or how many hours of rehearsals the Spring Musical really means. Know what you're getting yourself into and know where your personal limits lie.

How Much Time and Energy Are You Willing to Commit? Do You Have Availability to . . .

Help with Occasional Events?	Help in an Ongoing Way, but with a Limited Commitment?	Help at Certain Times of the Year?	Devote a Substantial Amount of Time?
If so, look at one-time events that require minimal preparation, like showing up to serve at a faculty lunch, chaperoning a field trip, or selling tickets at a concert.	If so, look at recurring activities or groups, like helping the school librarian shelve books one afternoon a week or joining a Friends of Music committee that meets once a month.	If so, look to connect your work to one-time events that require planning, like making costumes for a play, or to seasonal events, like being a volunteer coach.	If so, look at ongoing activities, like helping supervise students at lunch each day, joining a long-term committee with a significant time commitment, or running for public office.

www.ingramcontent.com/pod-product-compliance
Lightning Source LLC
Chambersburg PA
CBHW030139240426
43672CB00005B/184